The Art of
Kylie Johnston
Vol I.

www.kjarting.com

For my mother,
who lost her battle with
breast cancer on
November 20th, 2014.

She taught me how
to see the art in
everything.

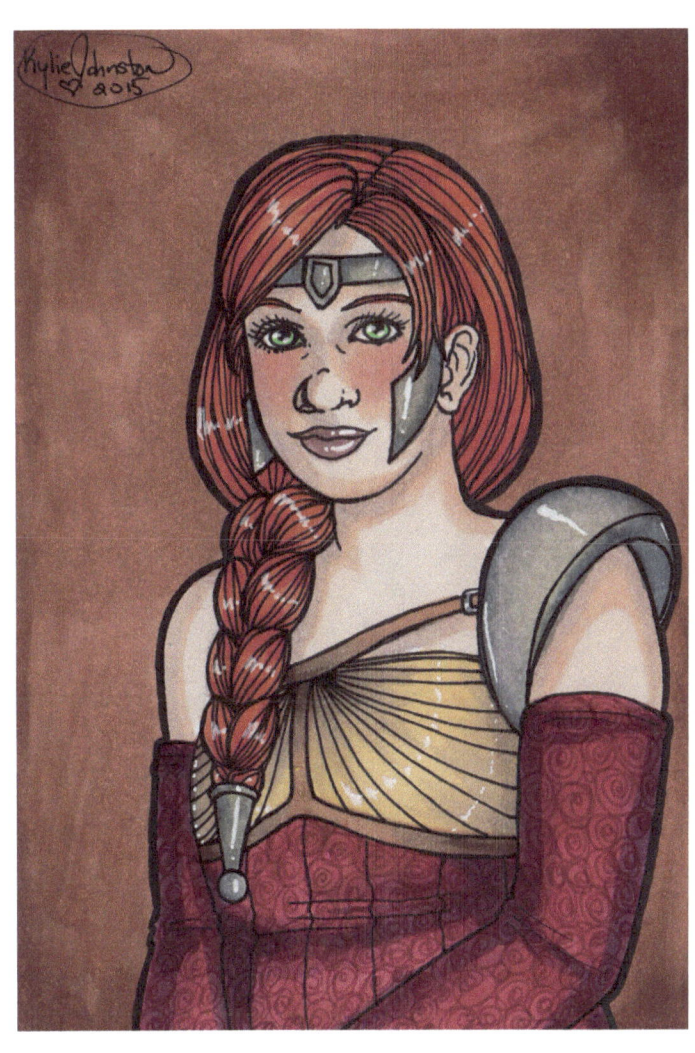

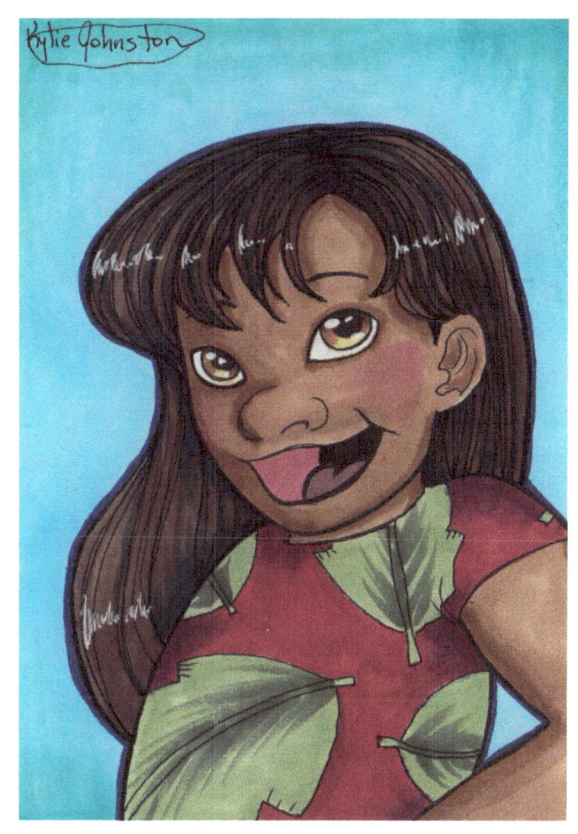

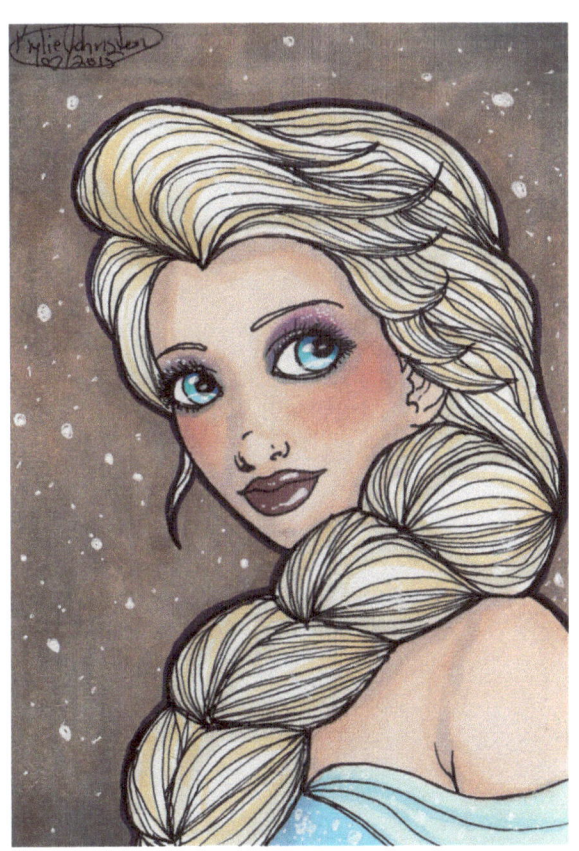

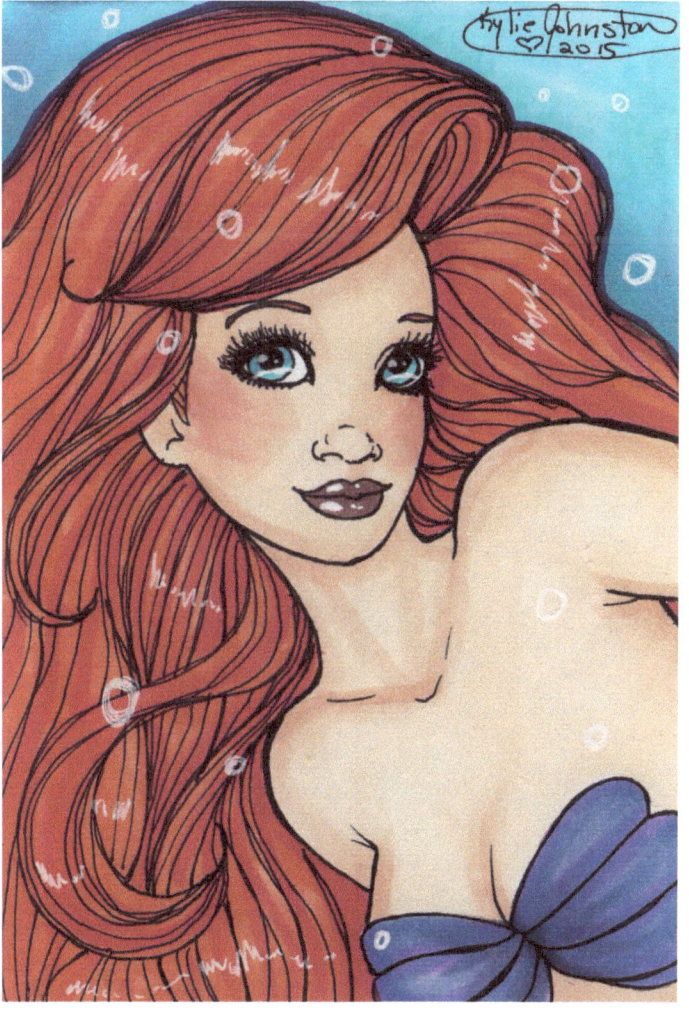

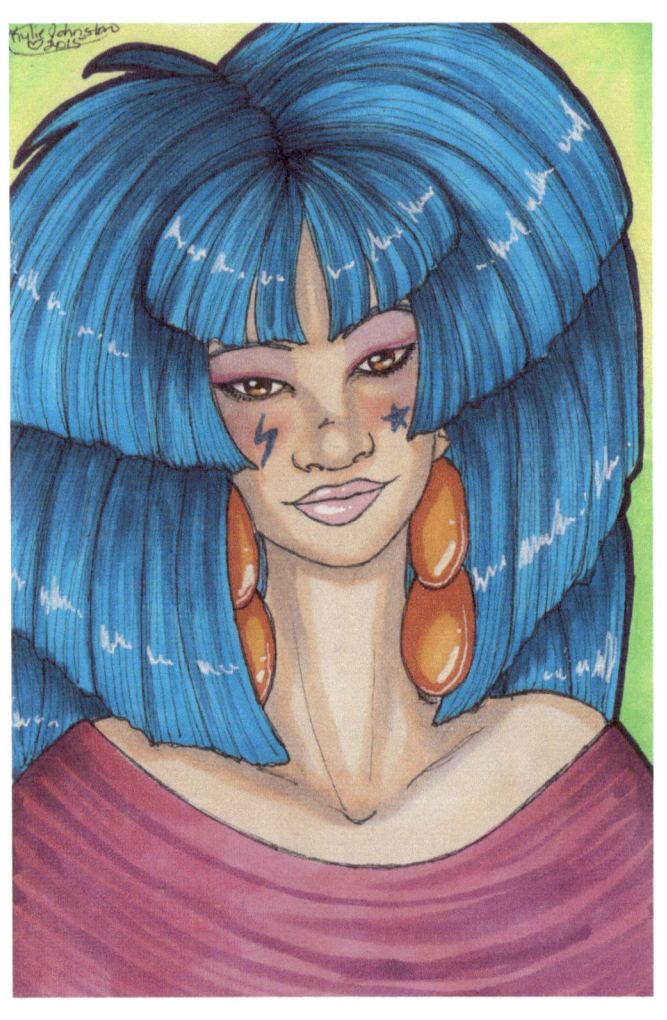
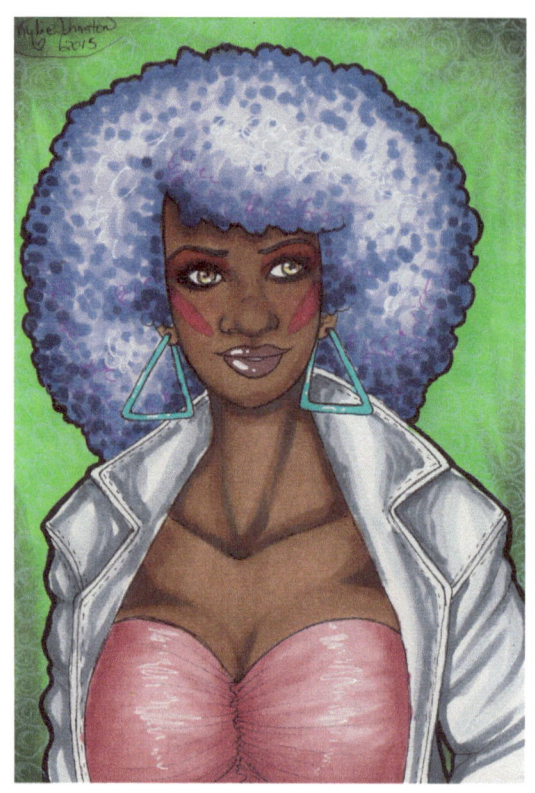
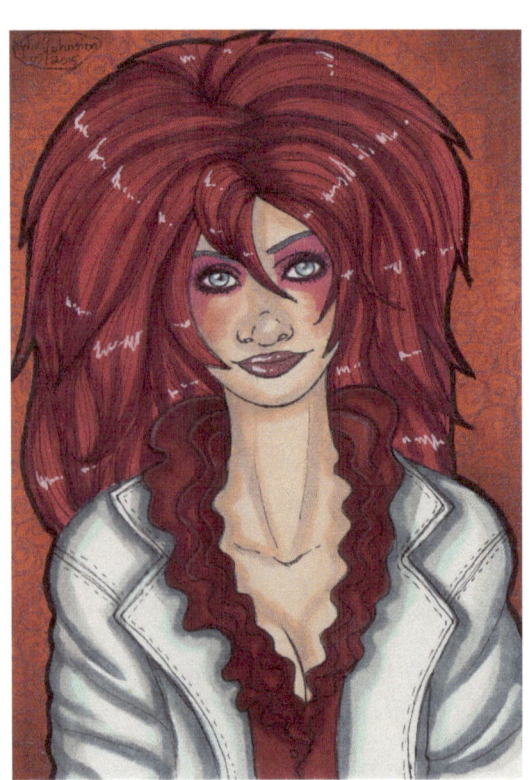
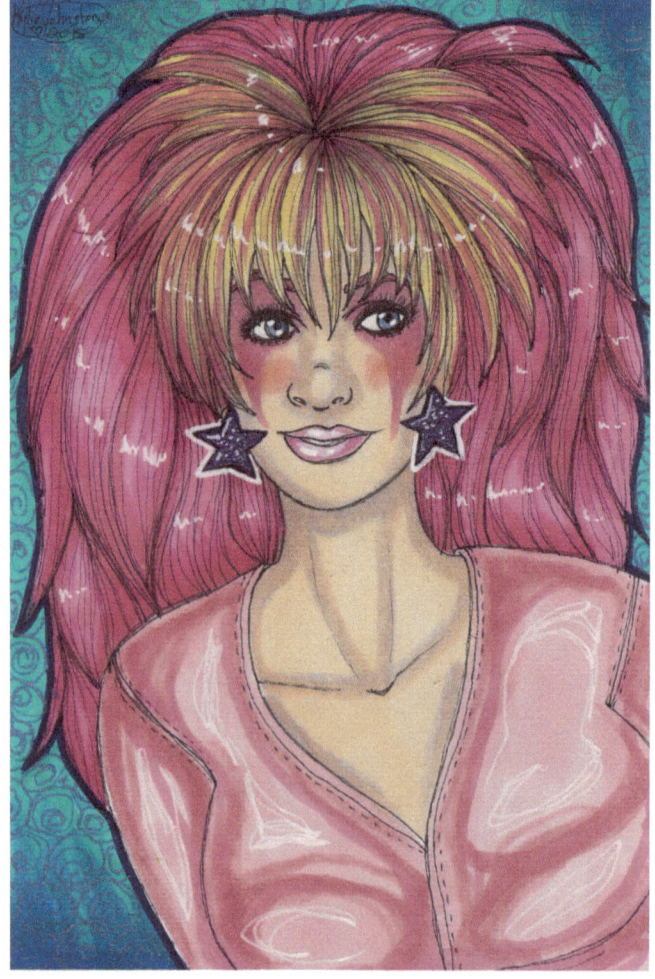

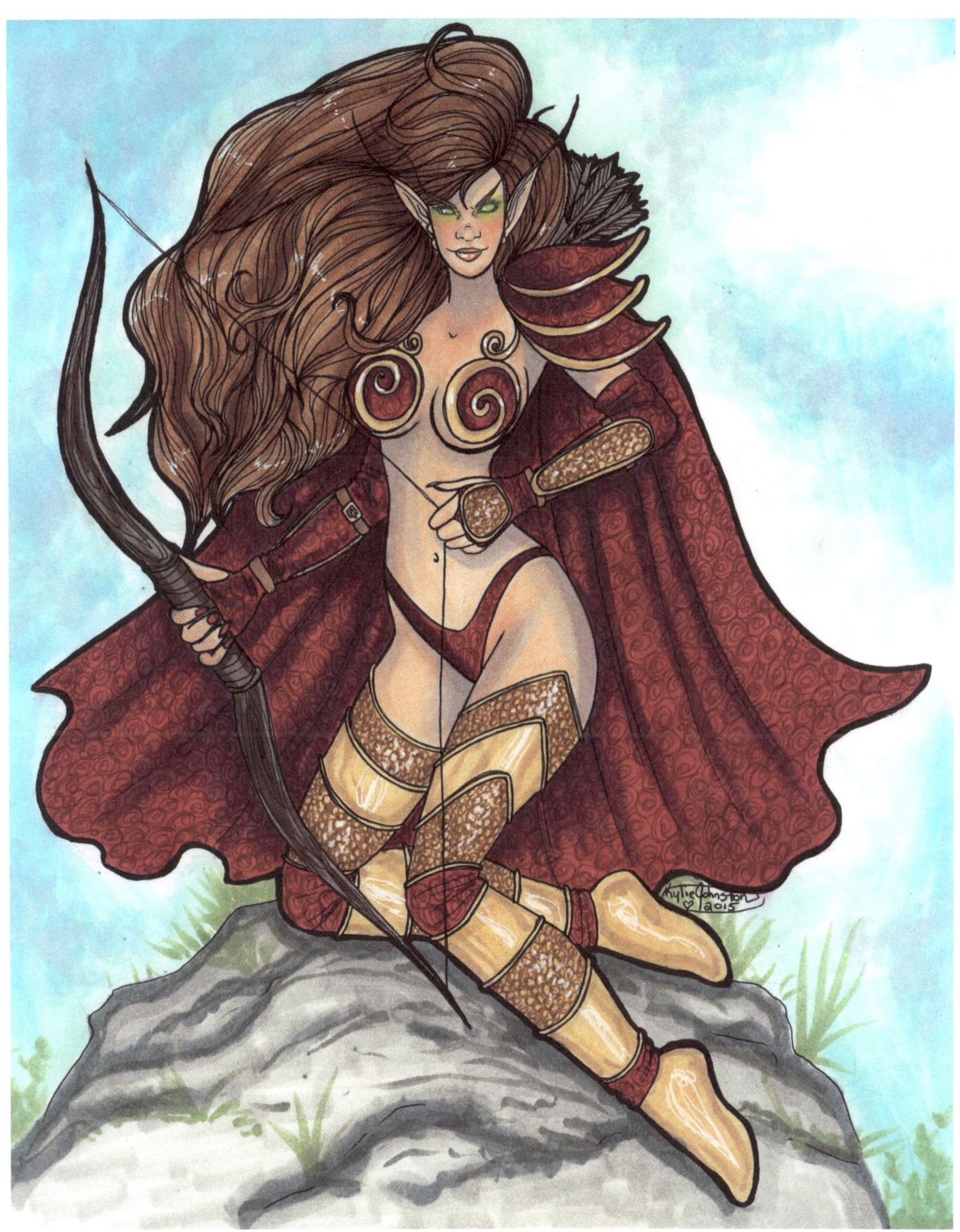

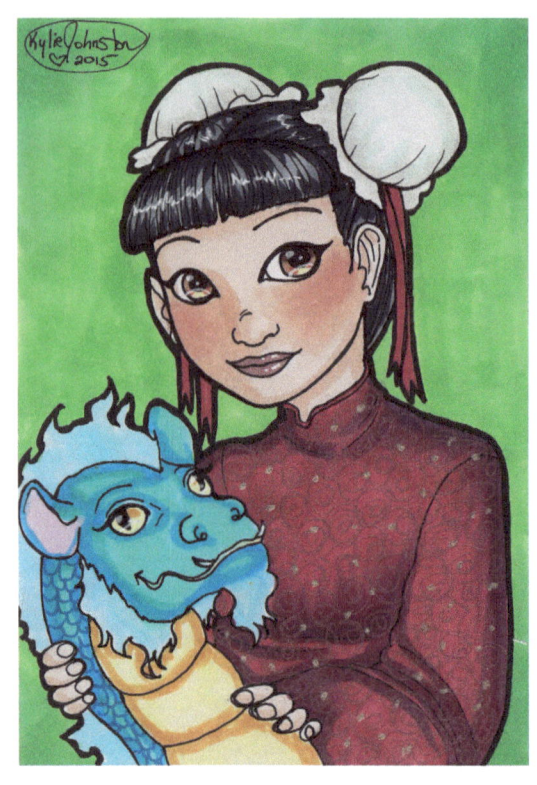
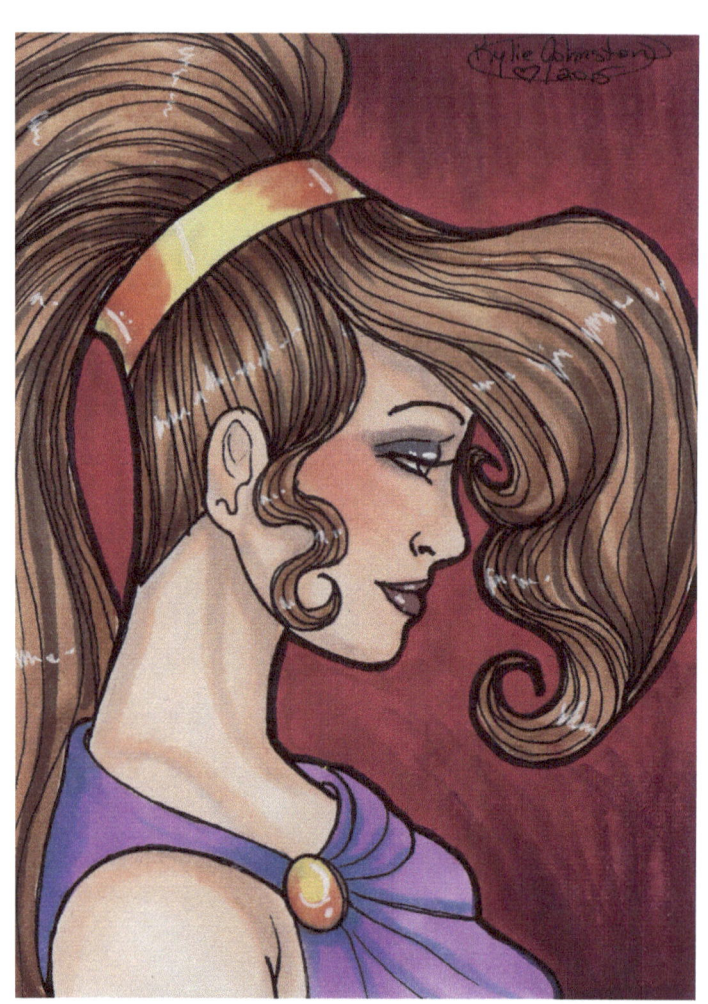
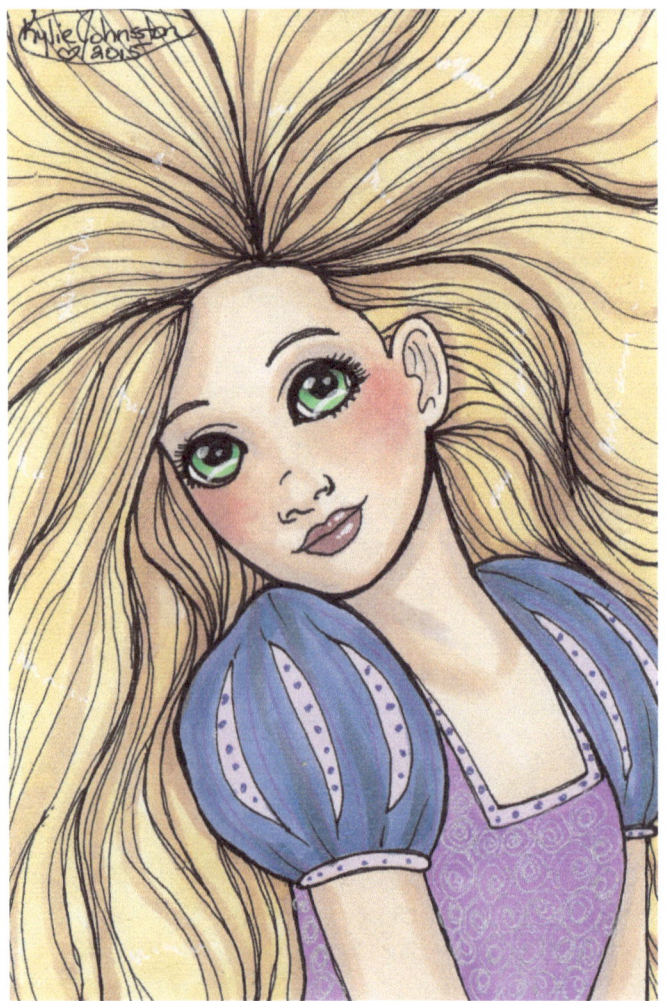
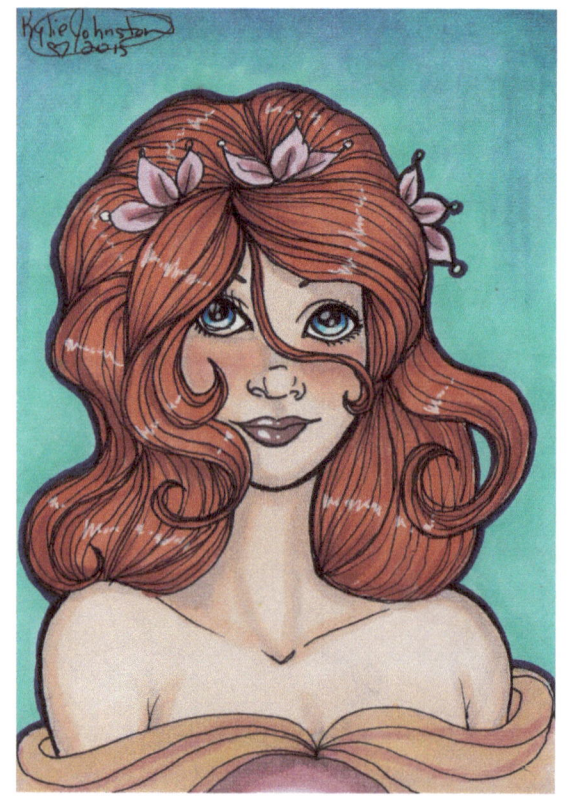

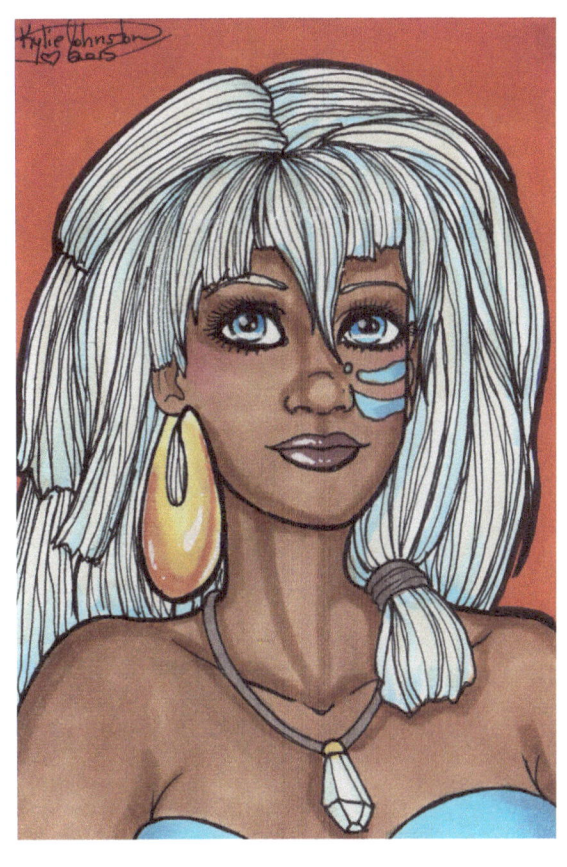
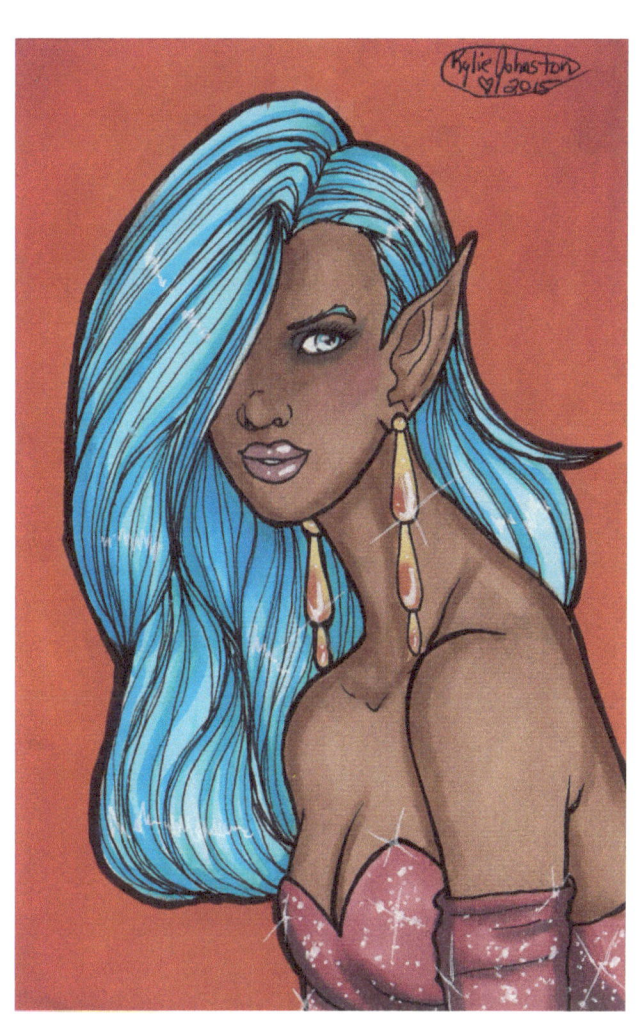
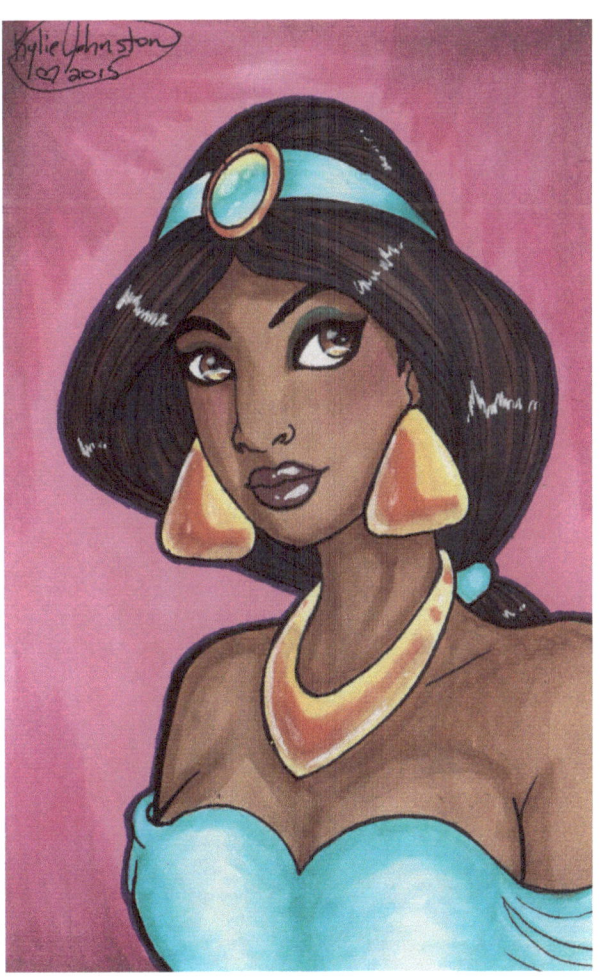
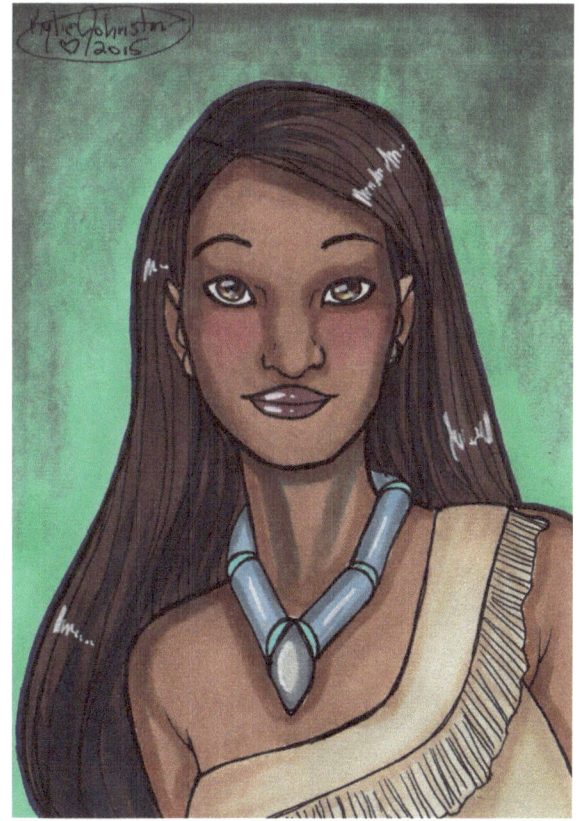

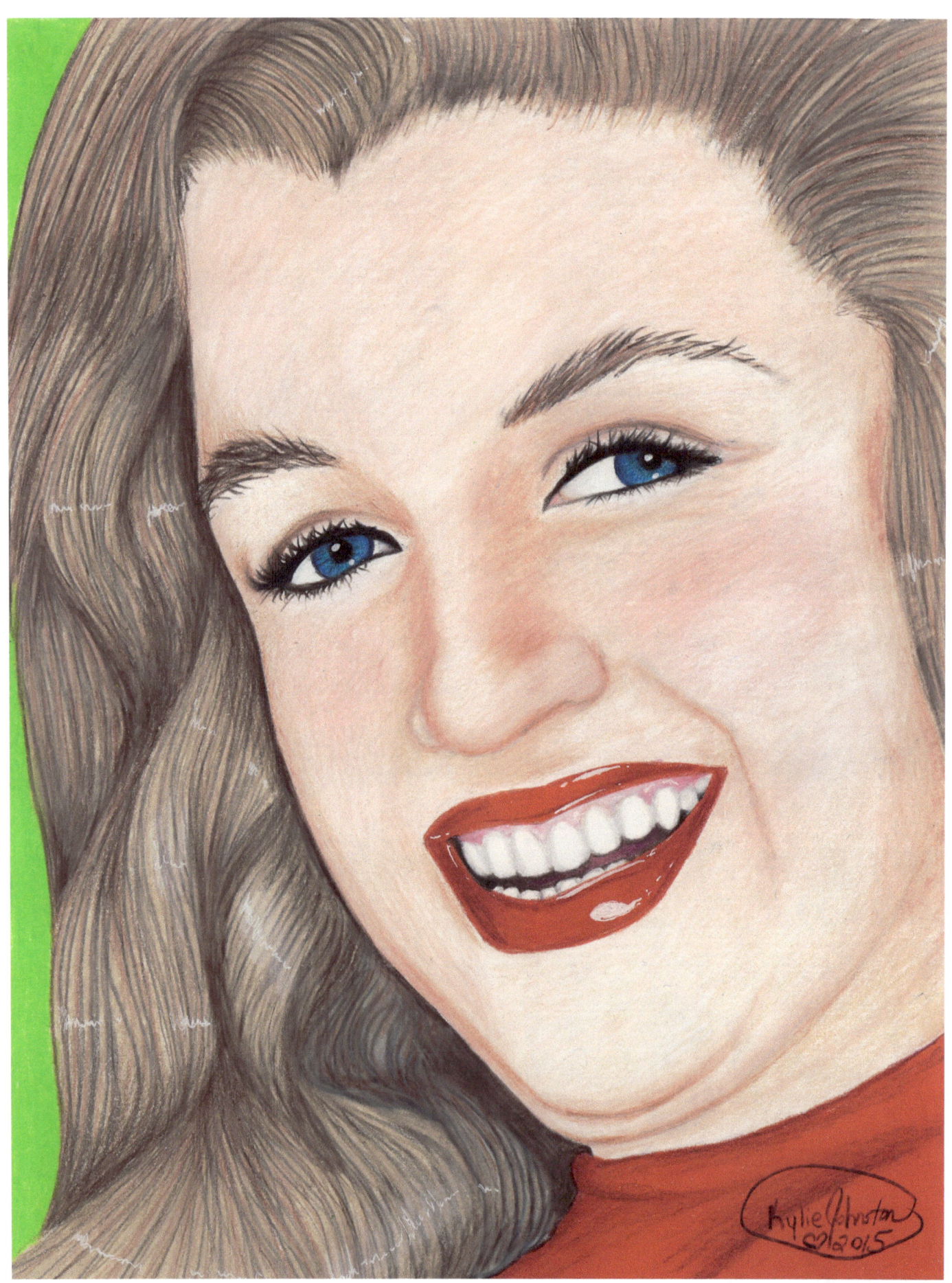

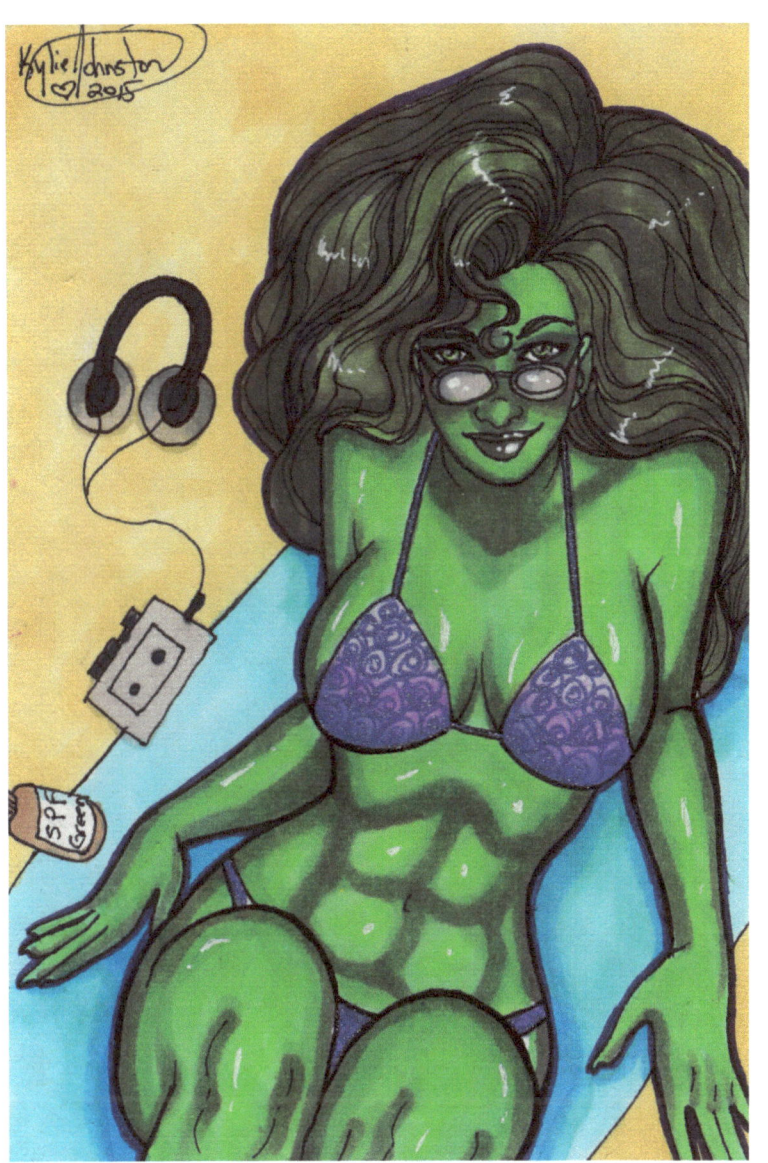
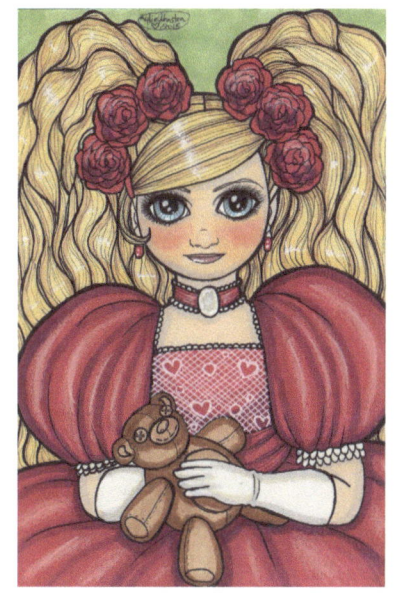
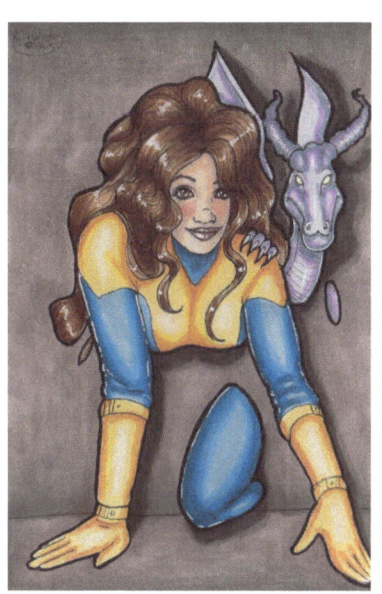
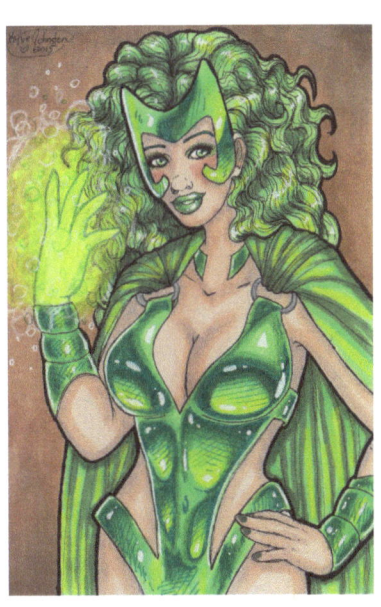
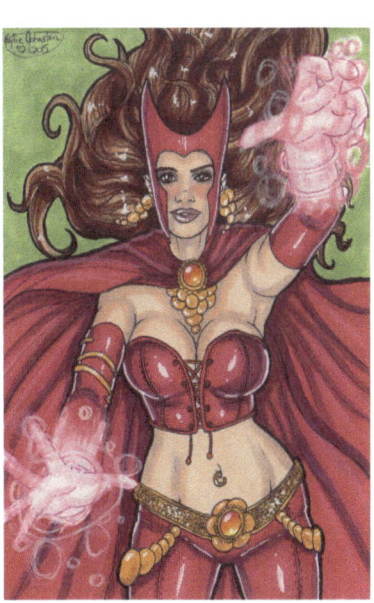

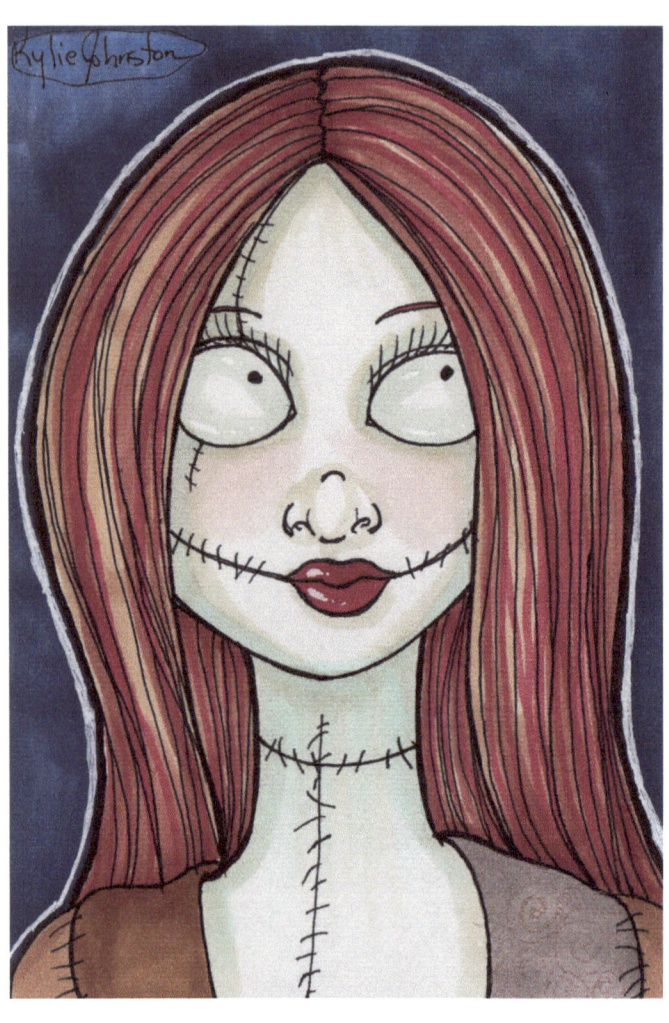

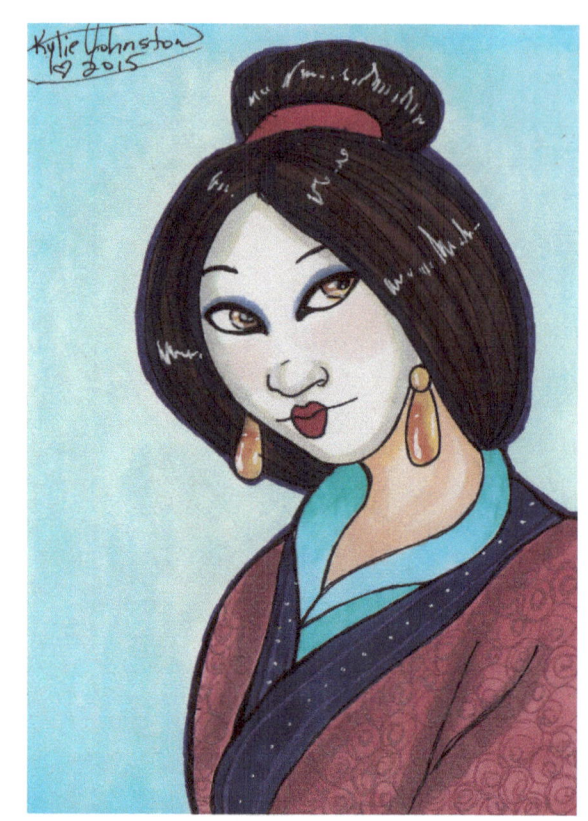

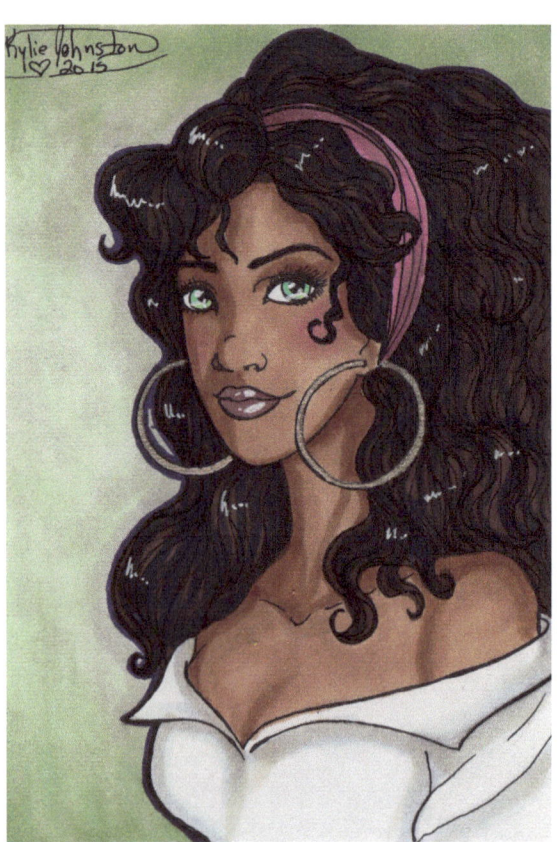

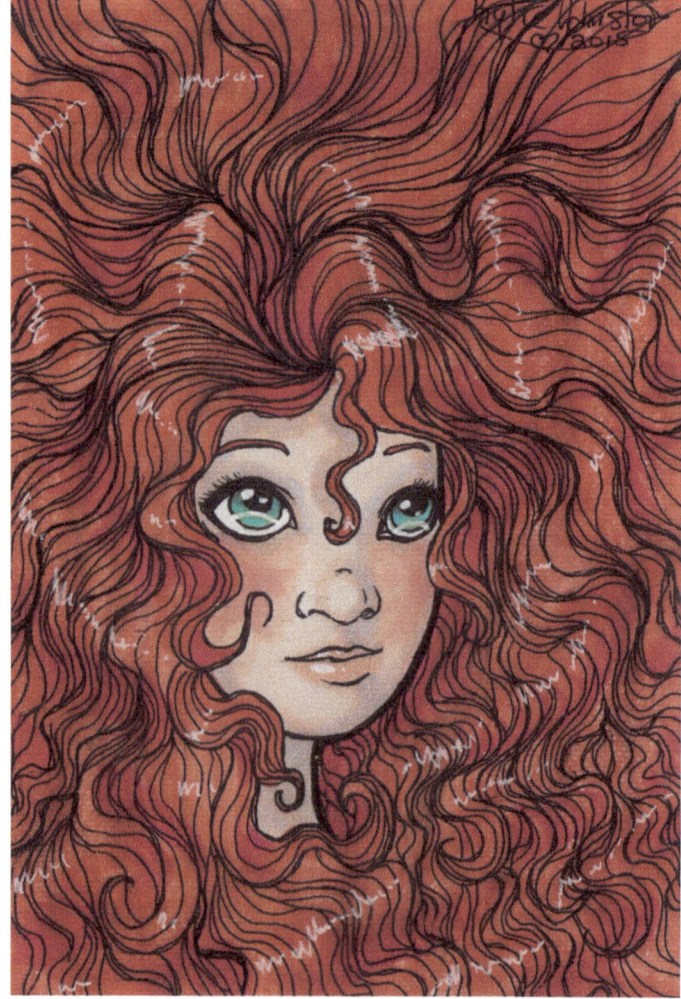

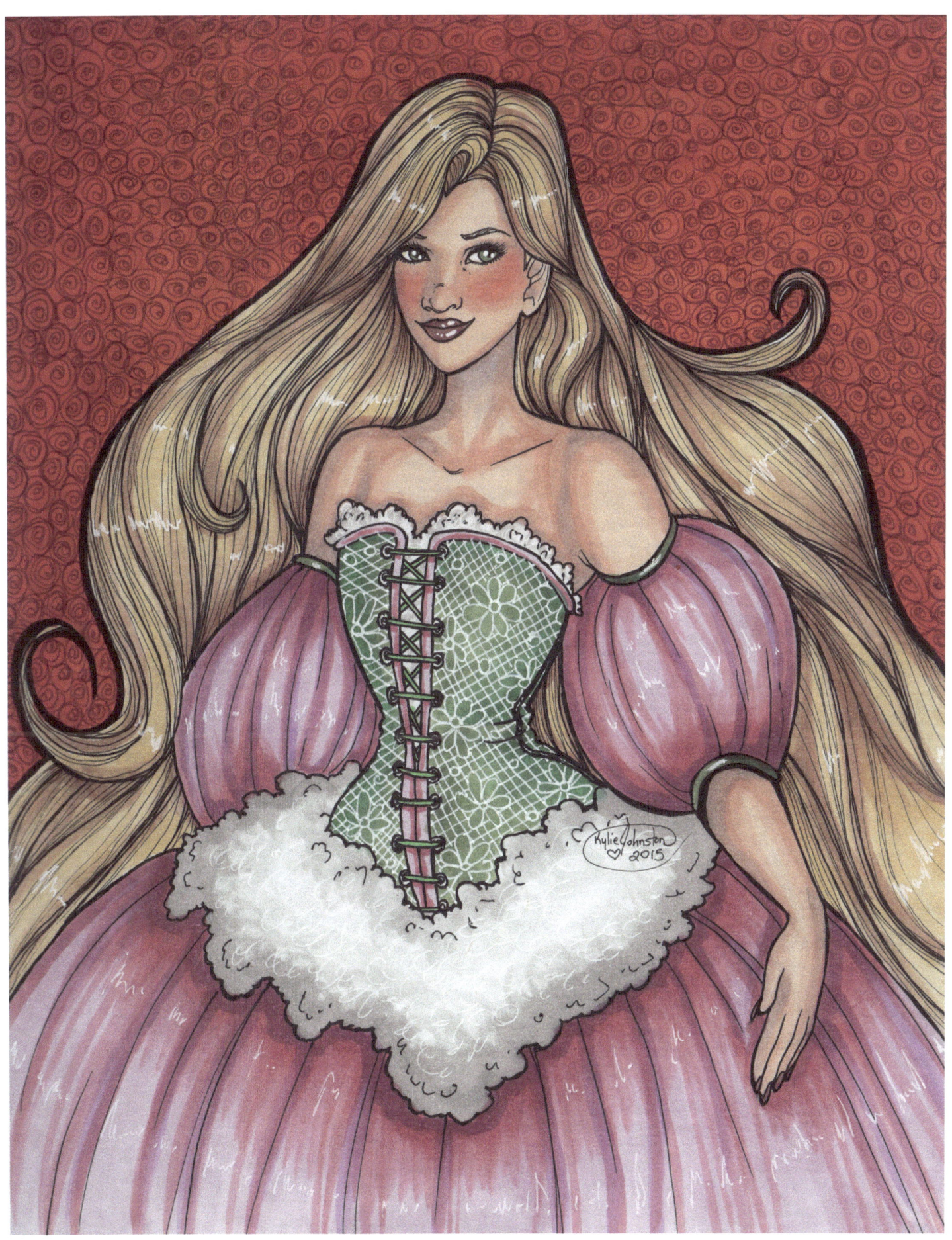

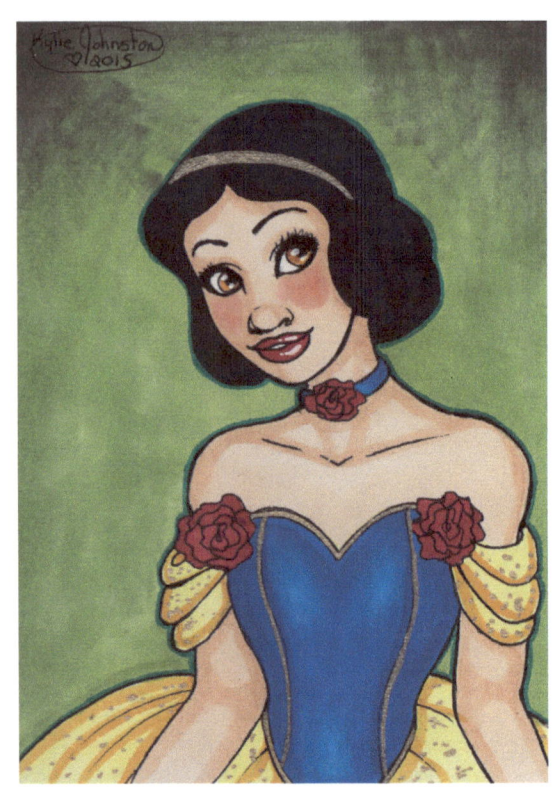

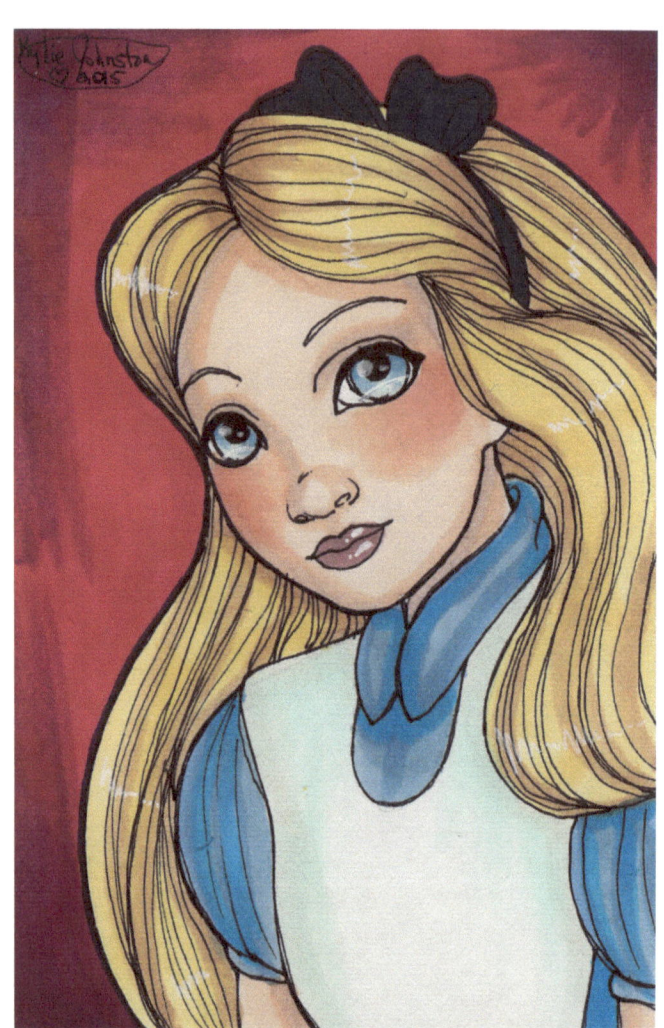

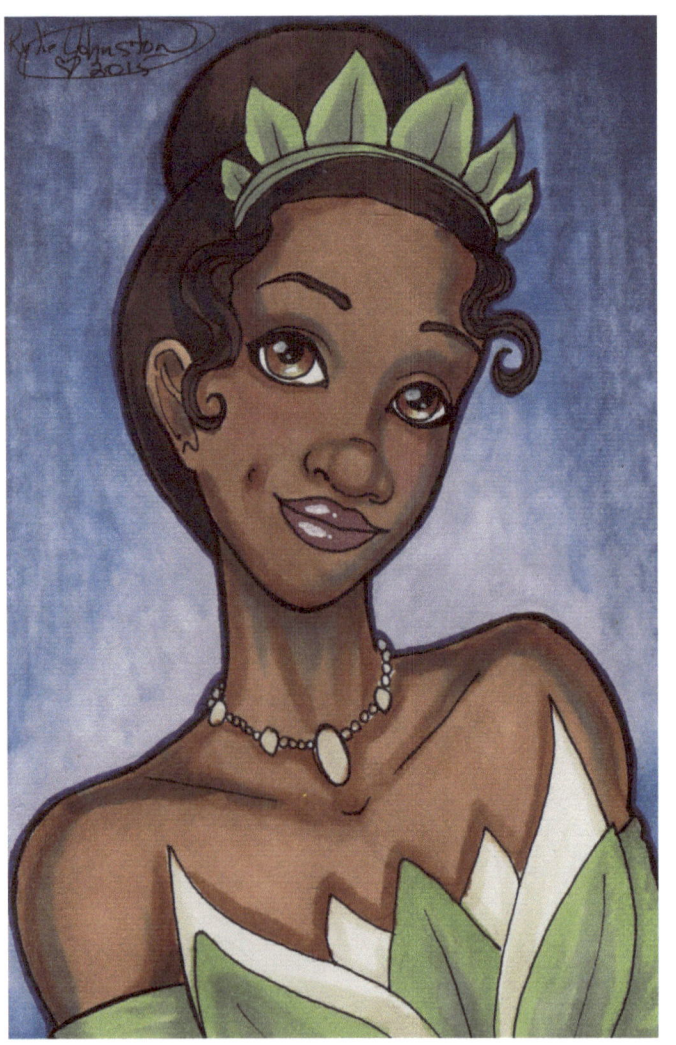

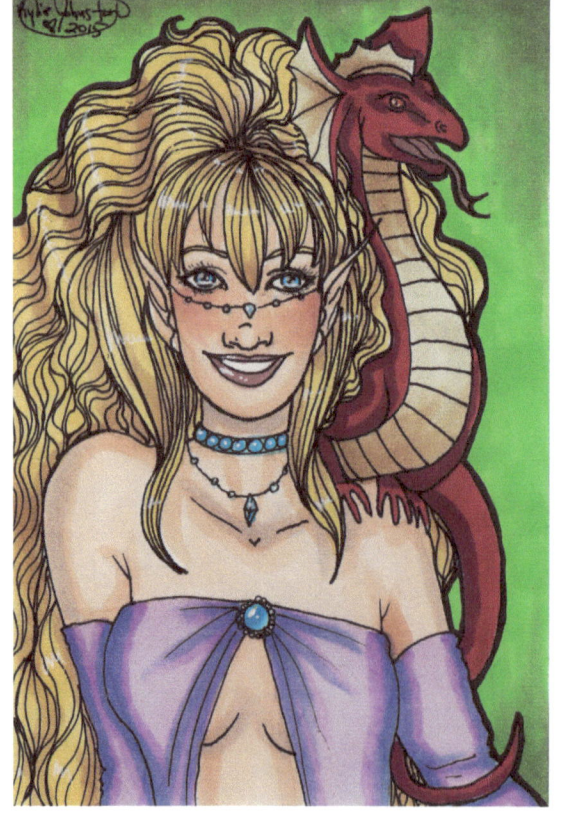

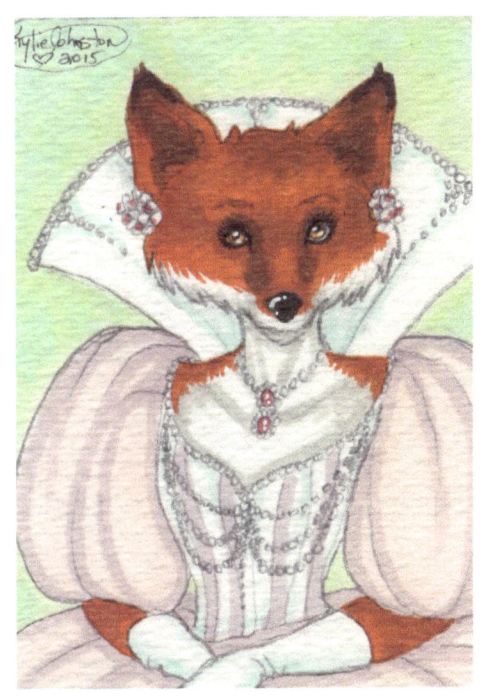
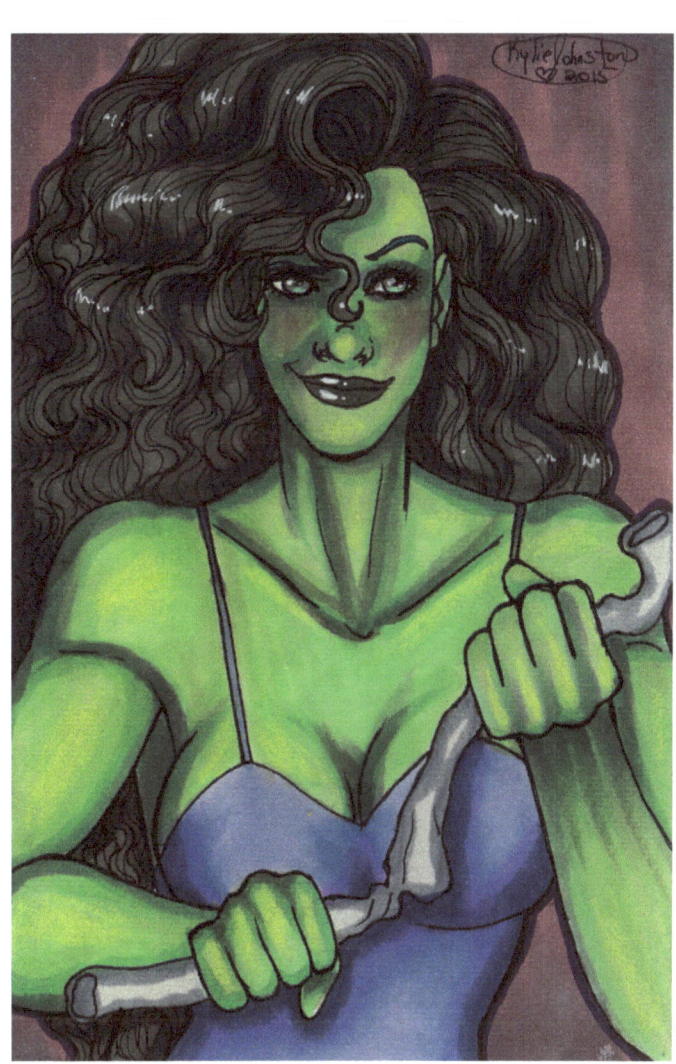
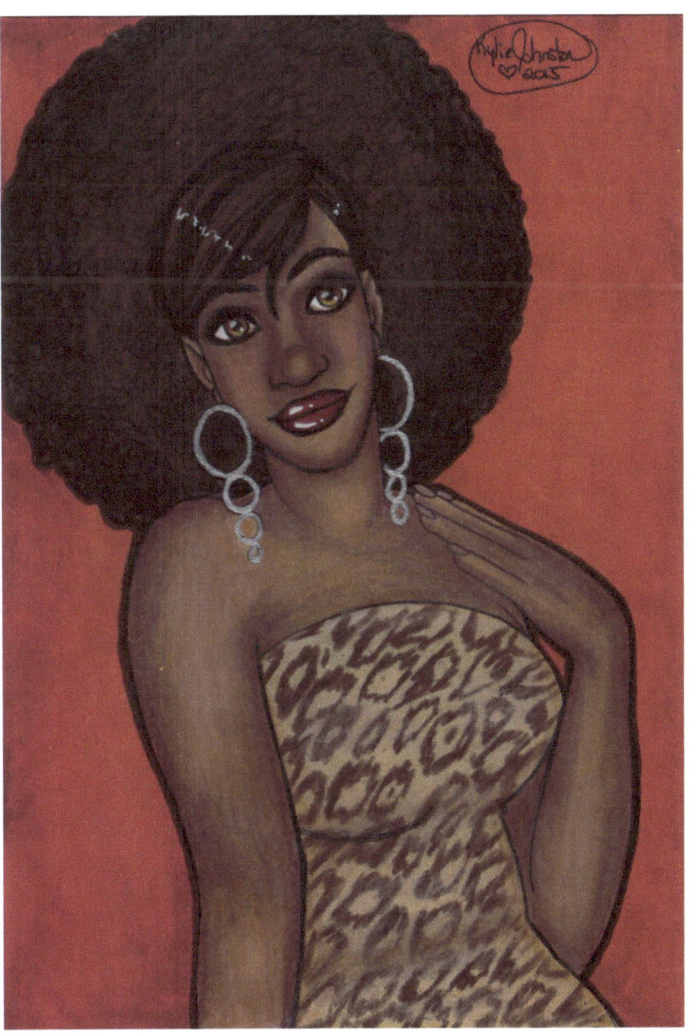
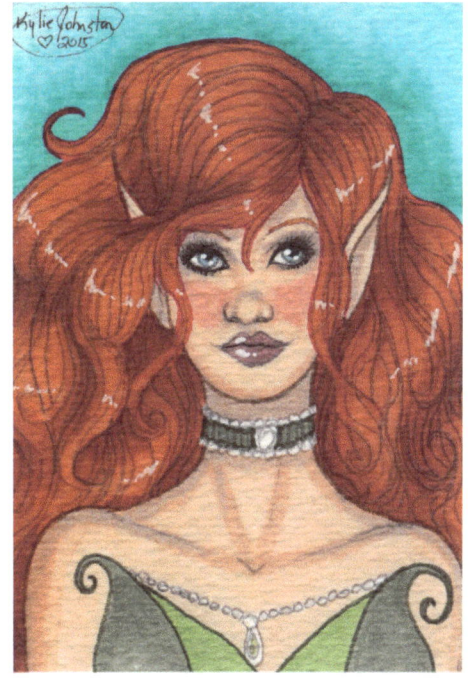

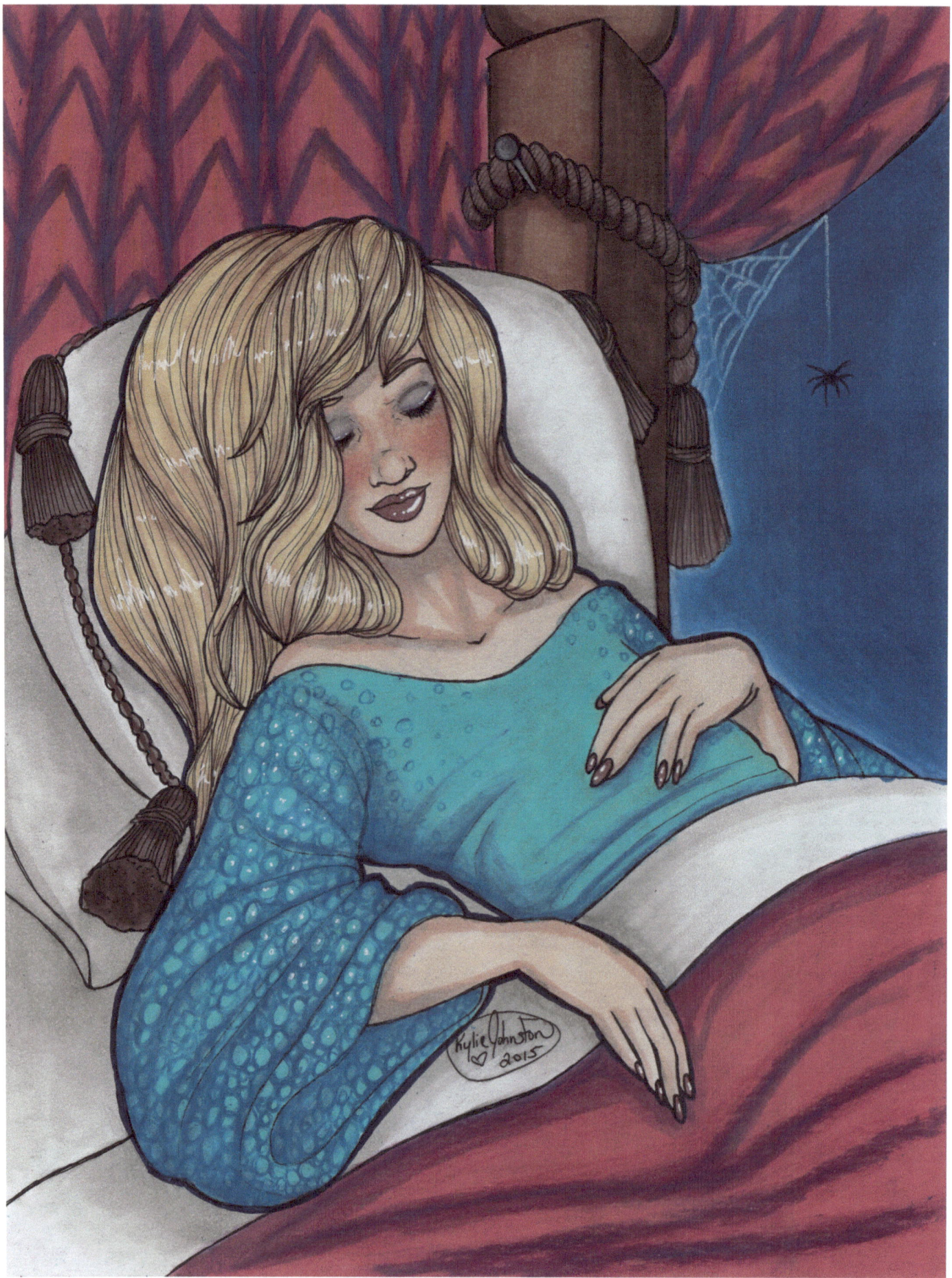

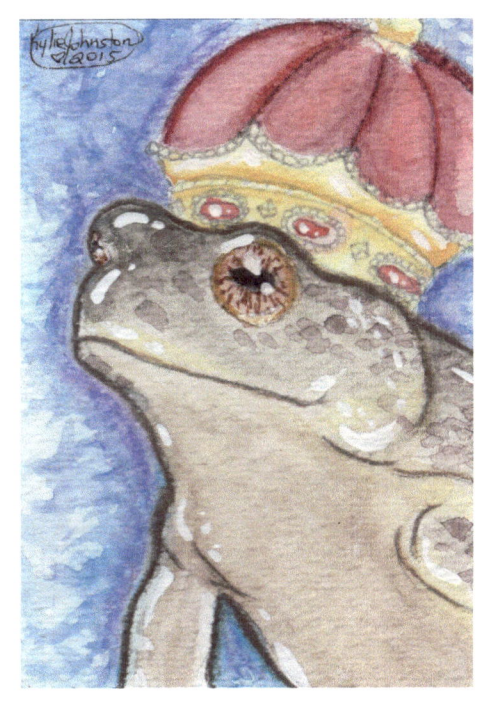
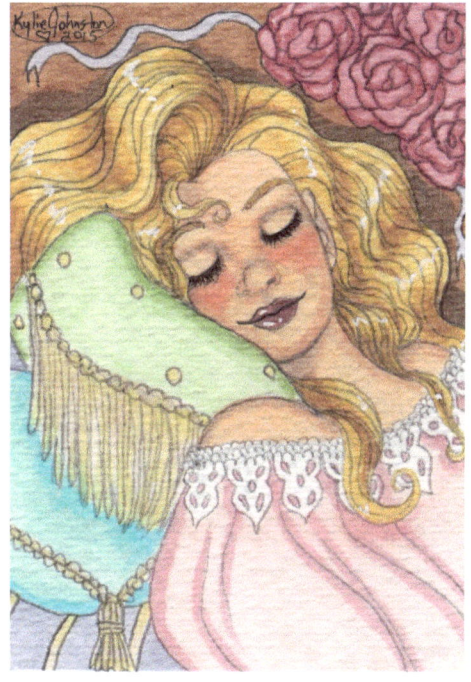
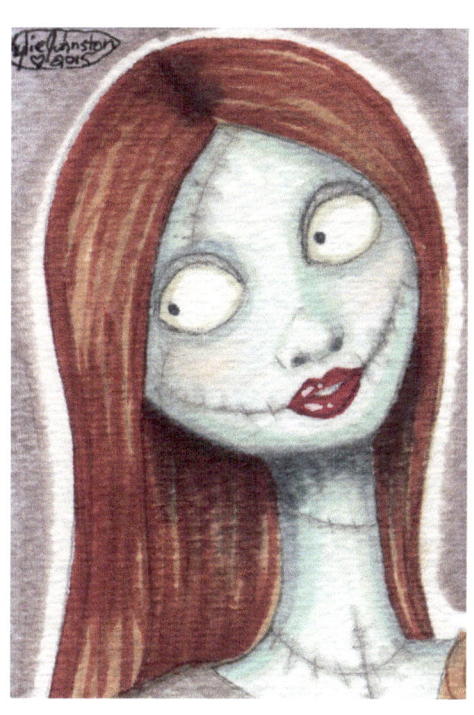
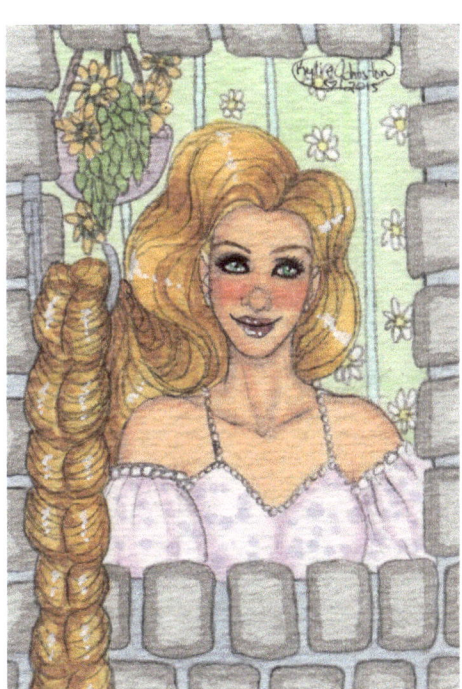
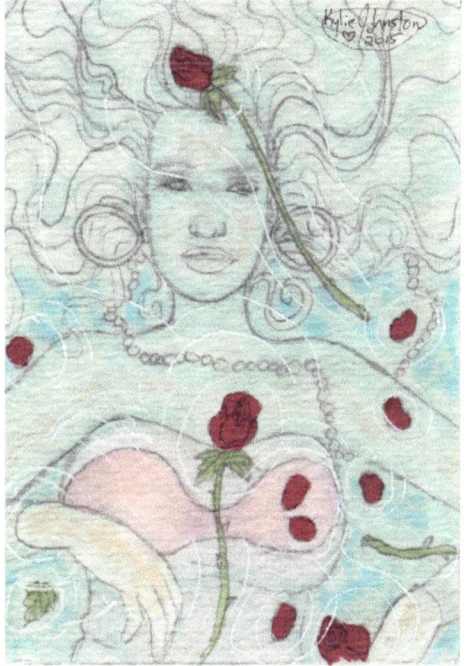
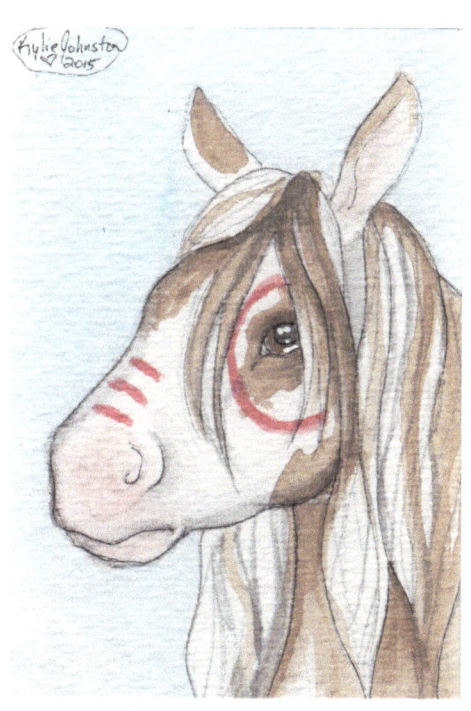

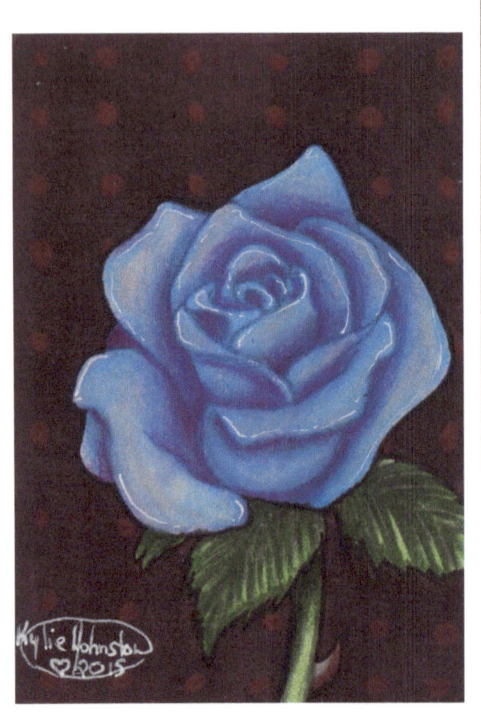
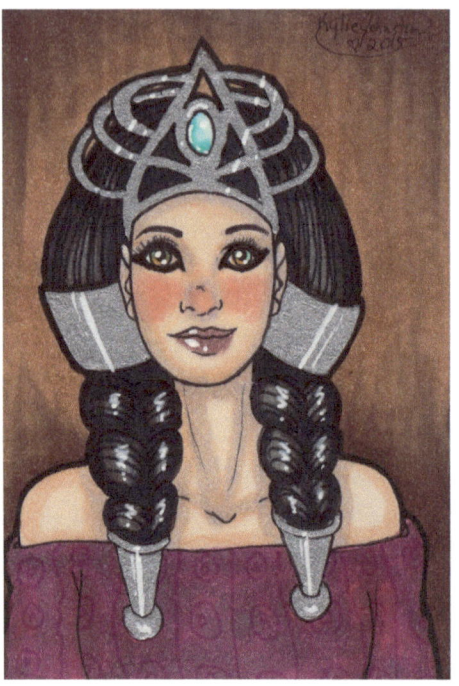
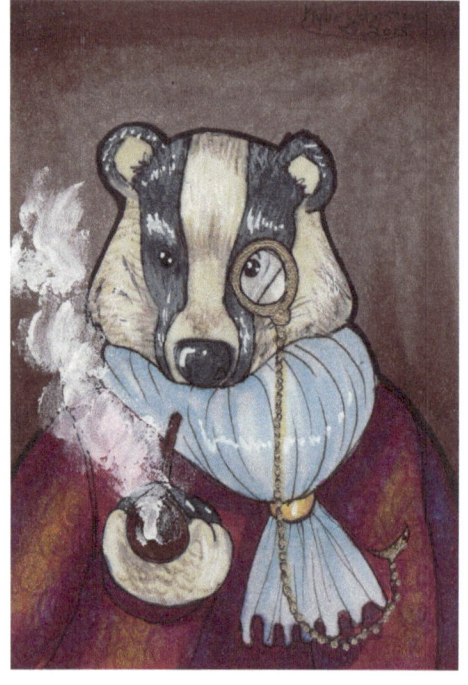
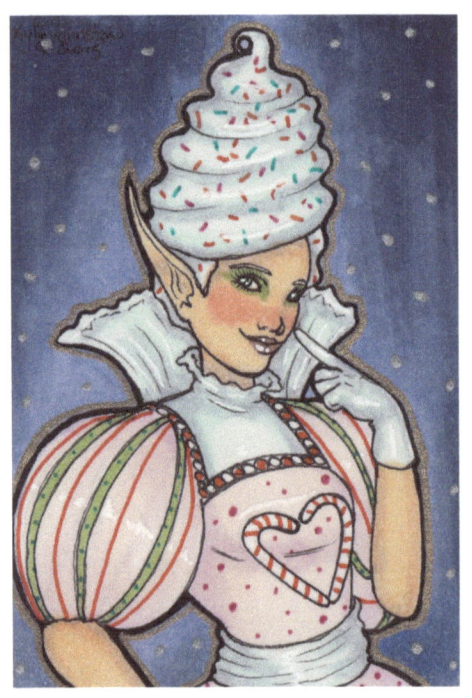
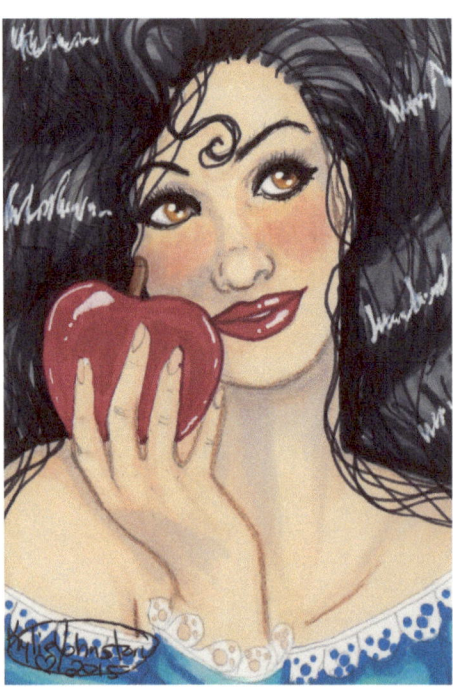
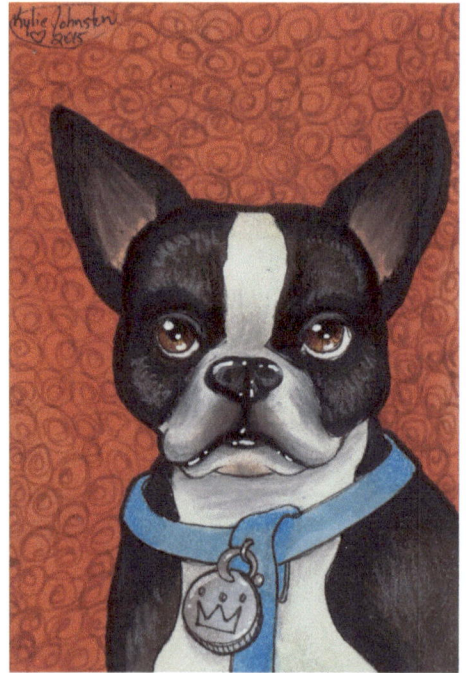

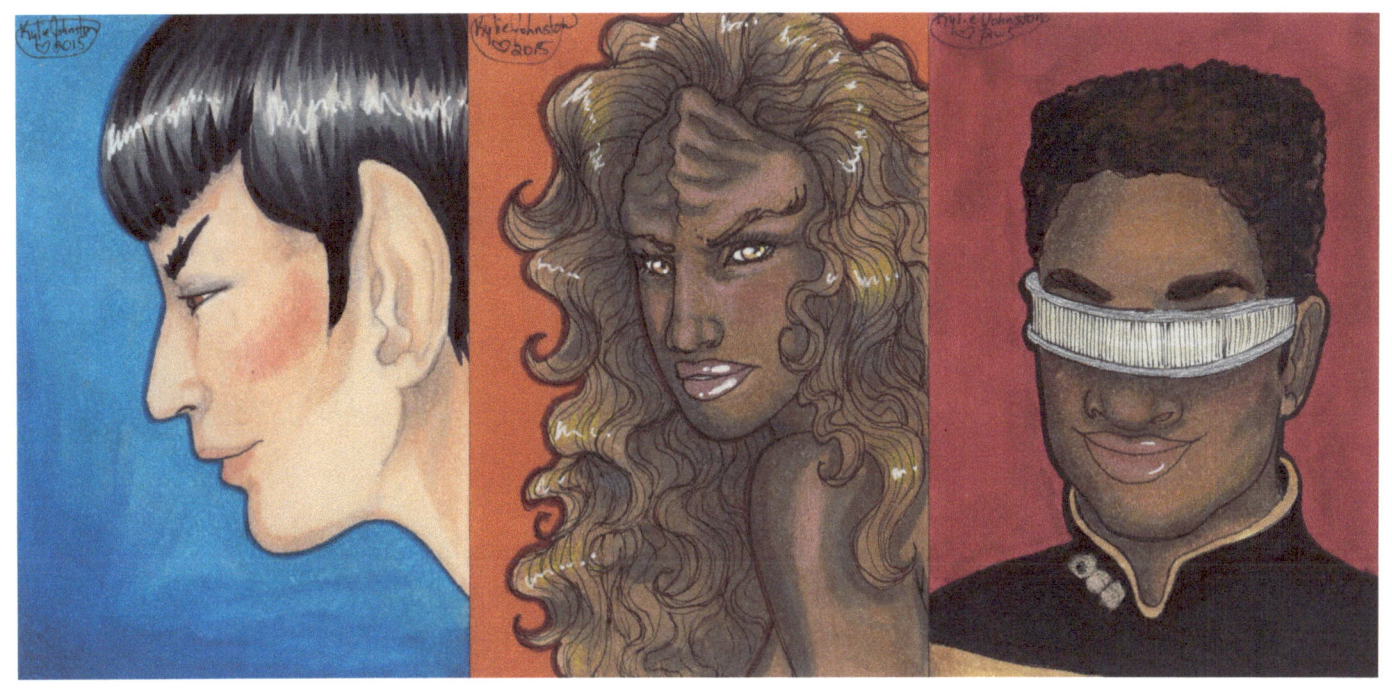
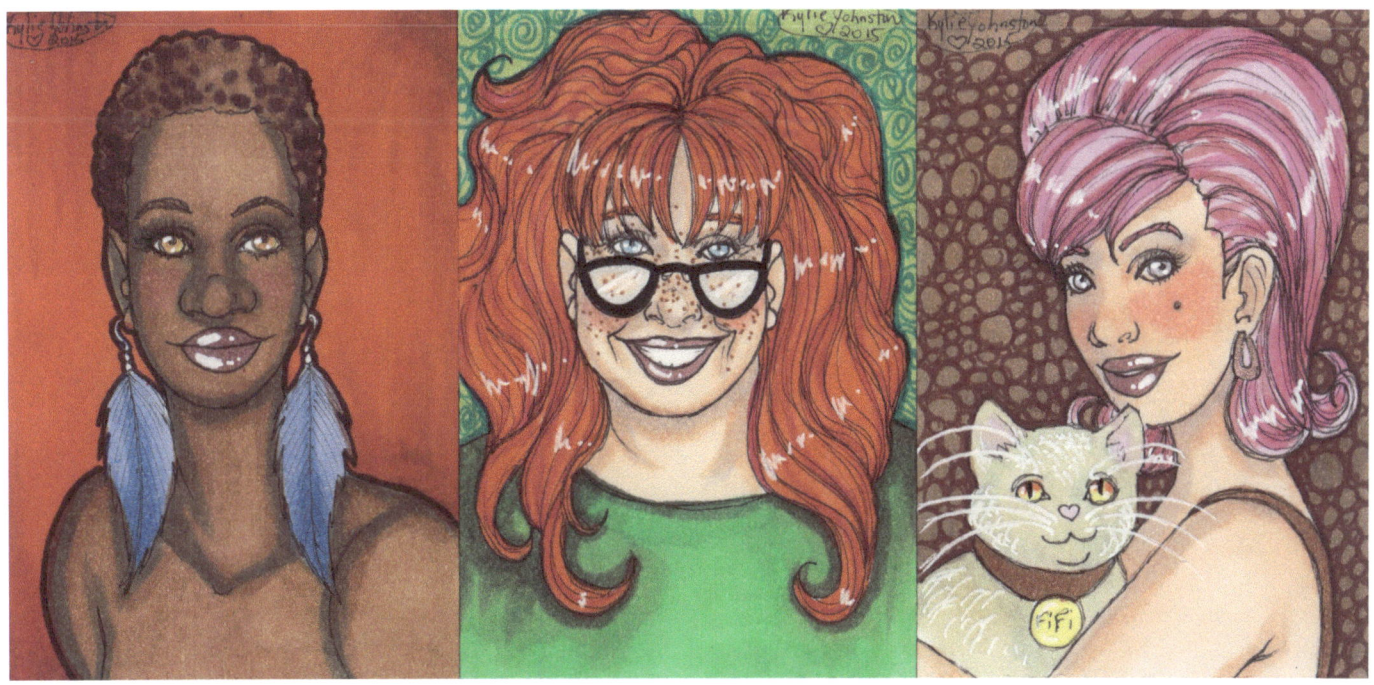

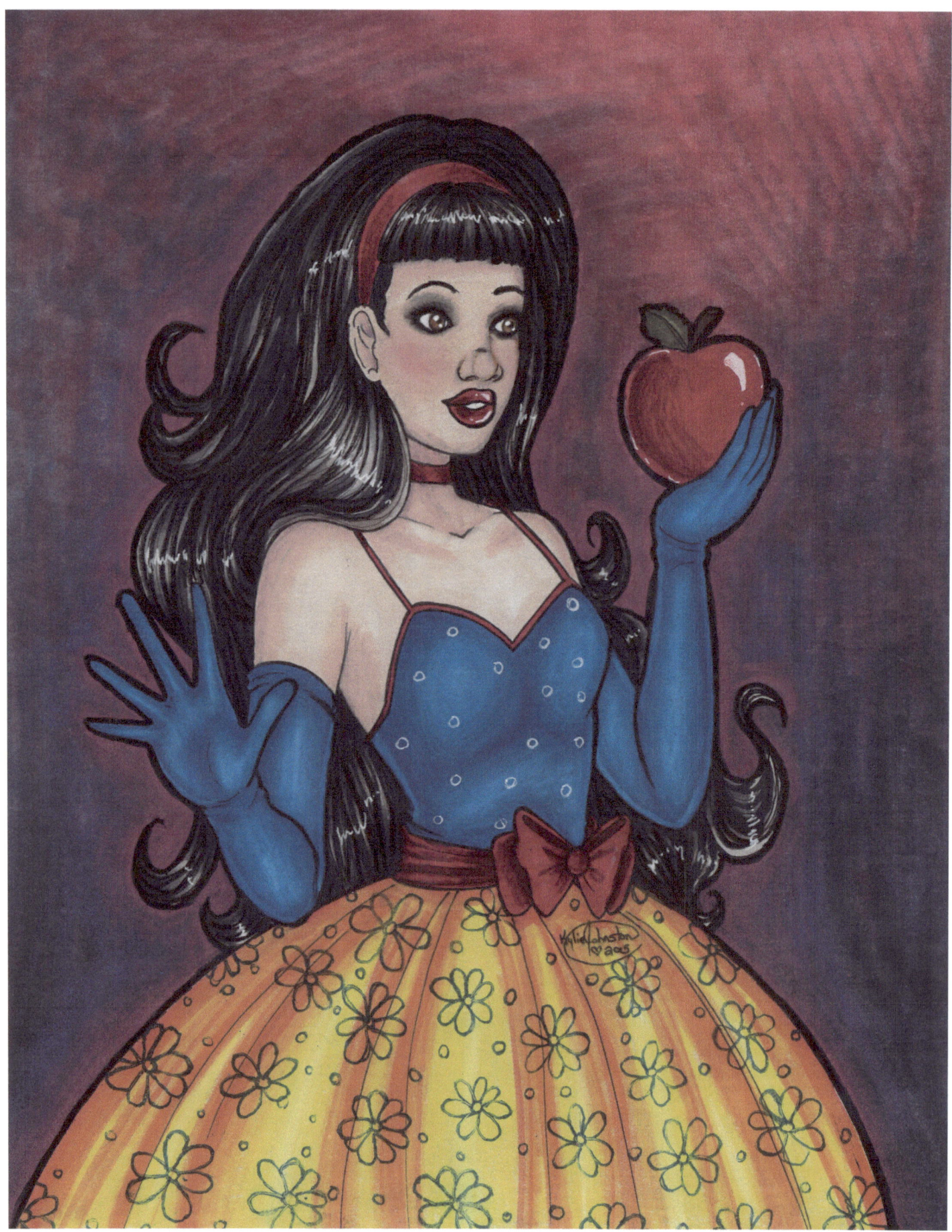

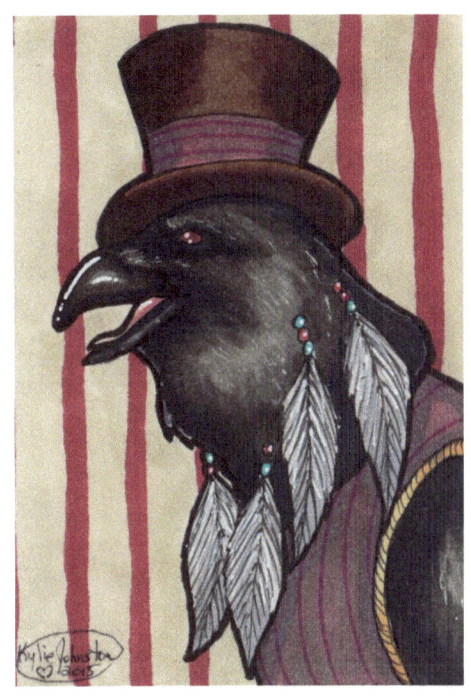
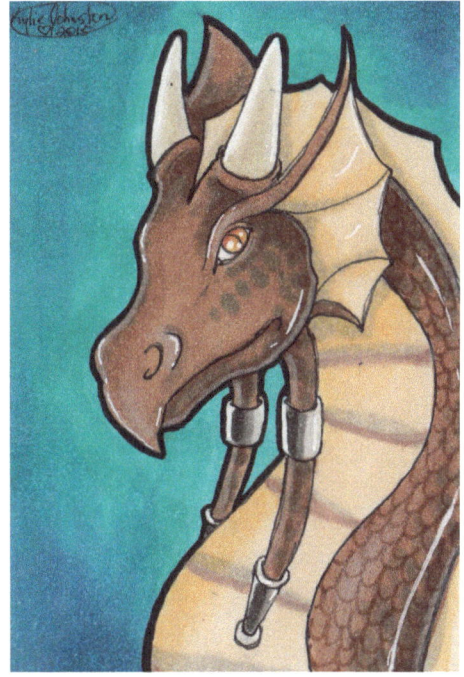
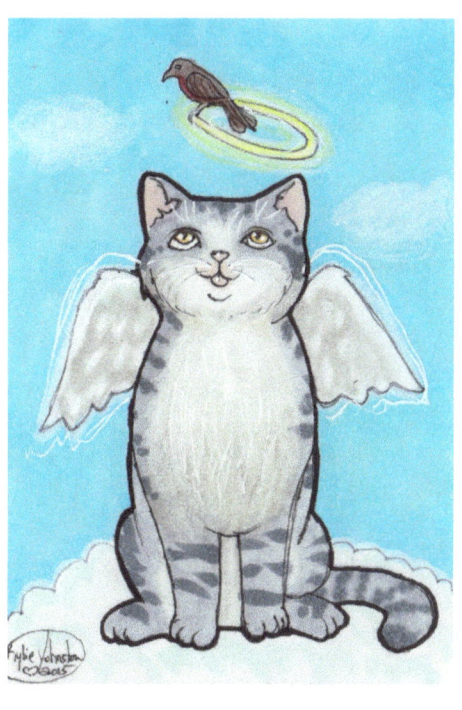
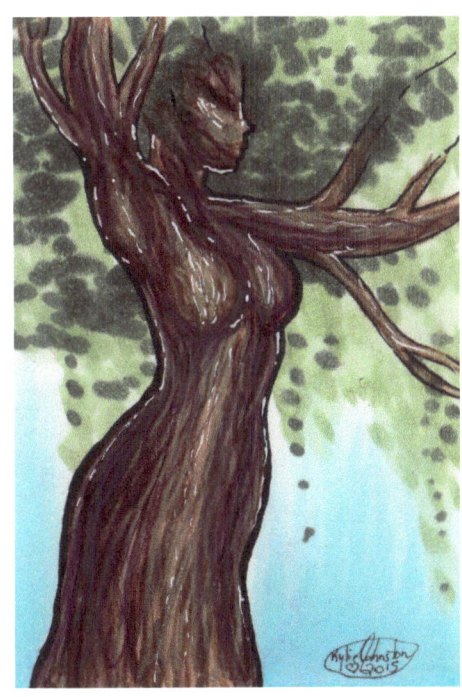
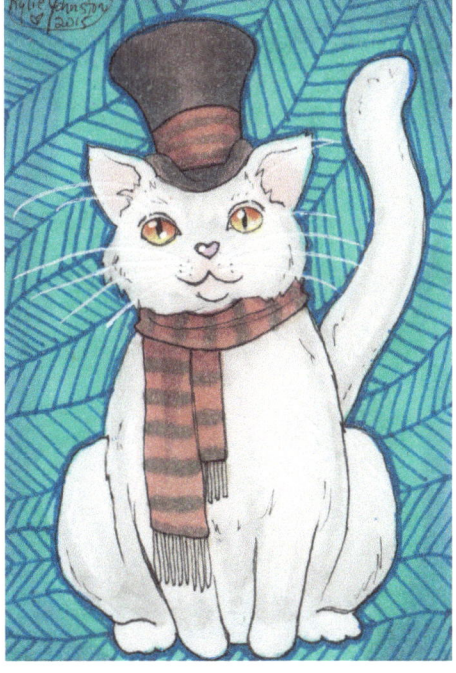
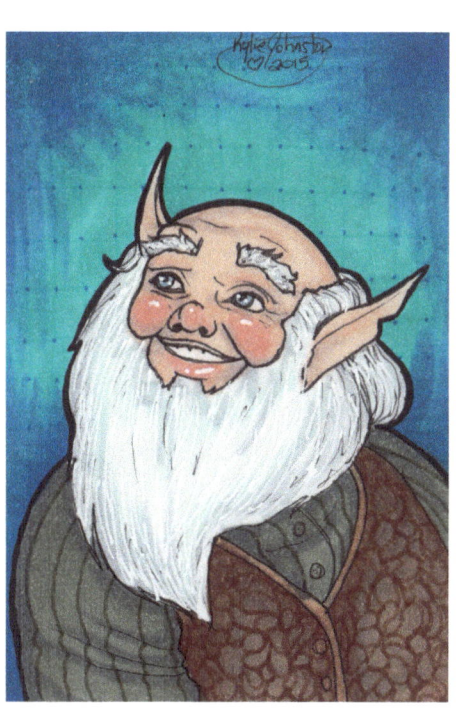

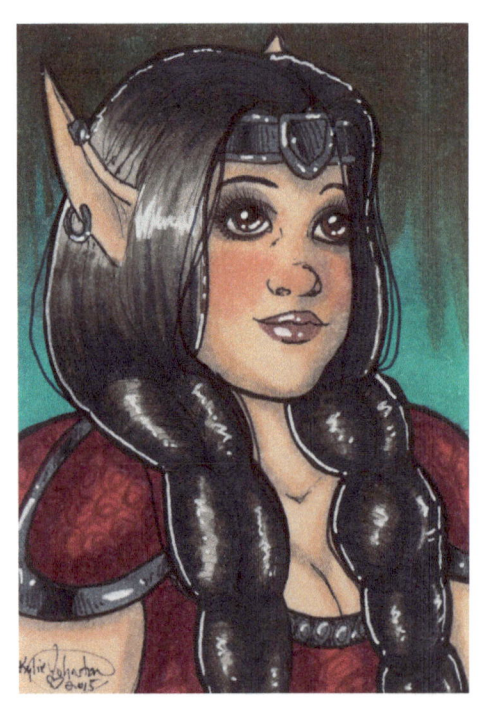
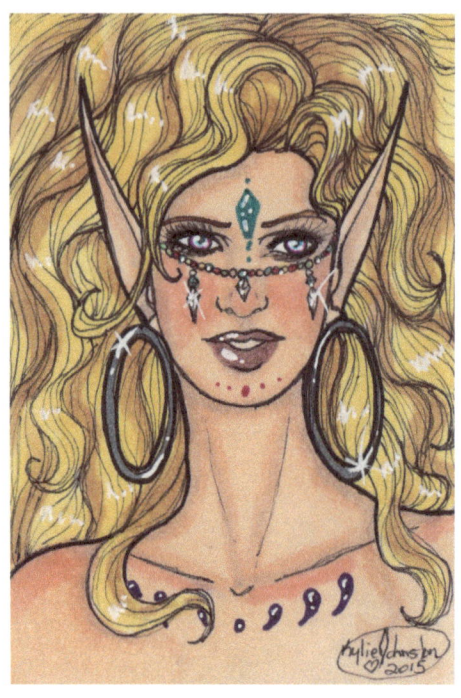
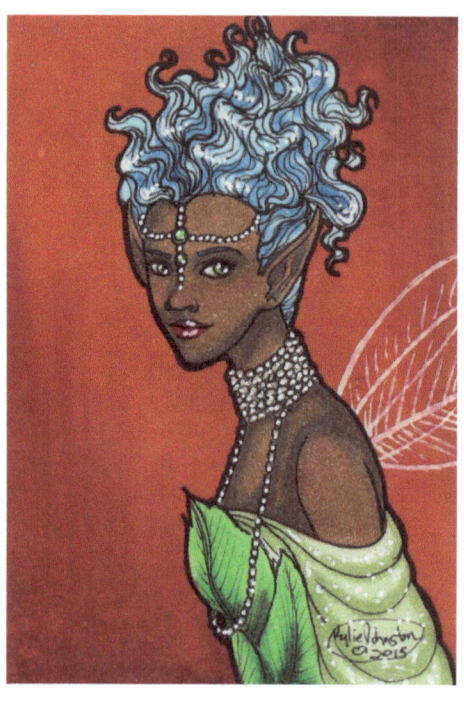
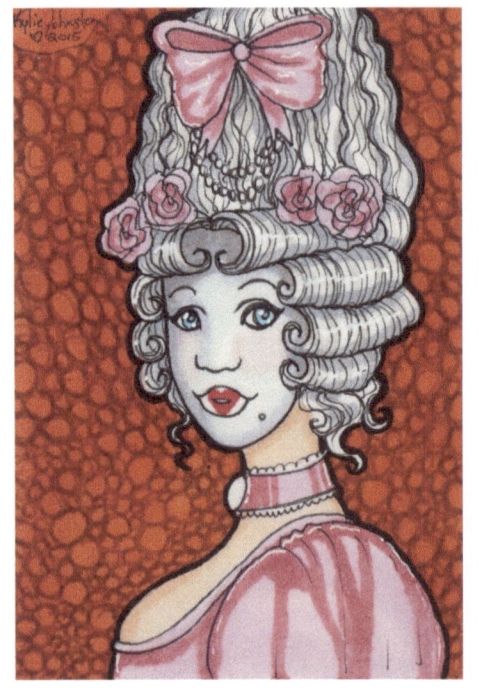
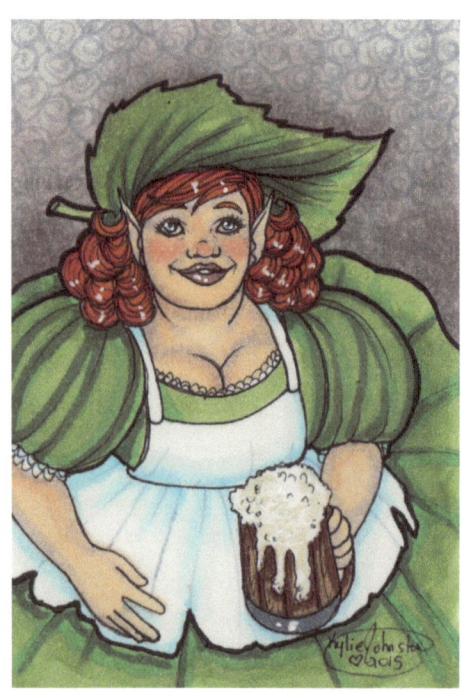
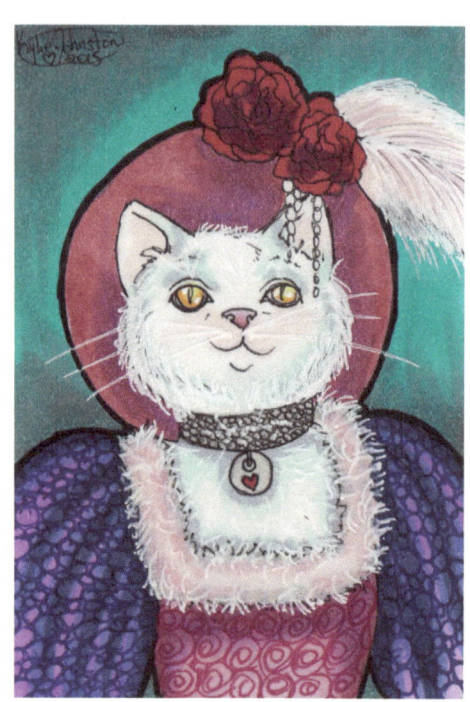

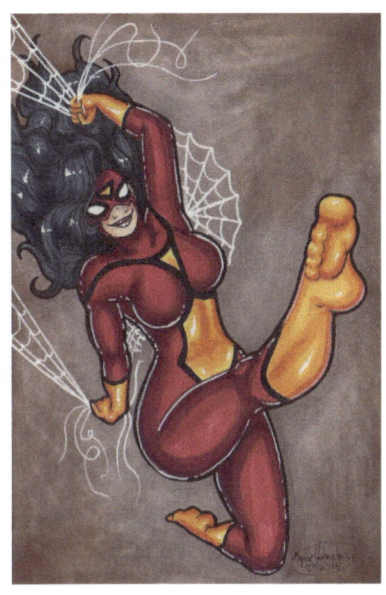

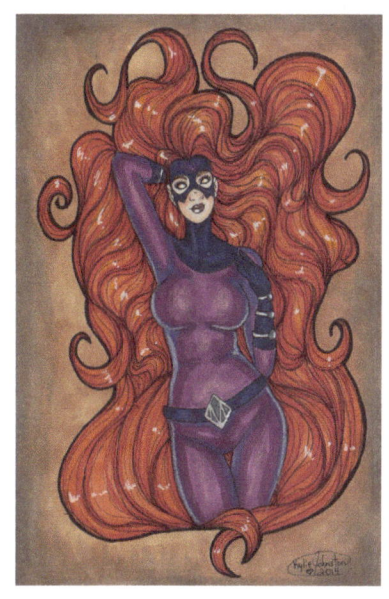

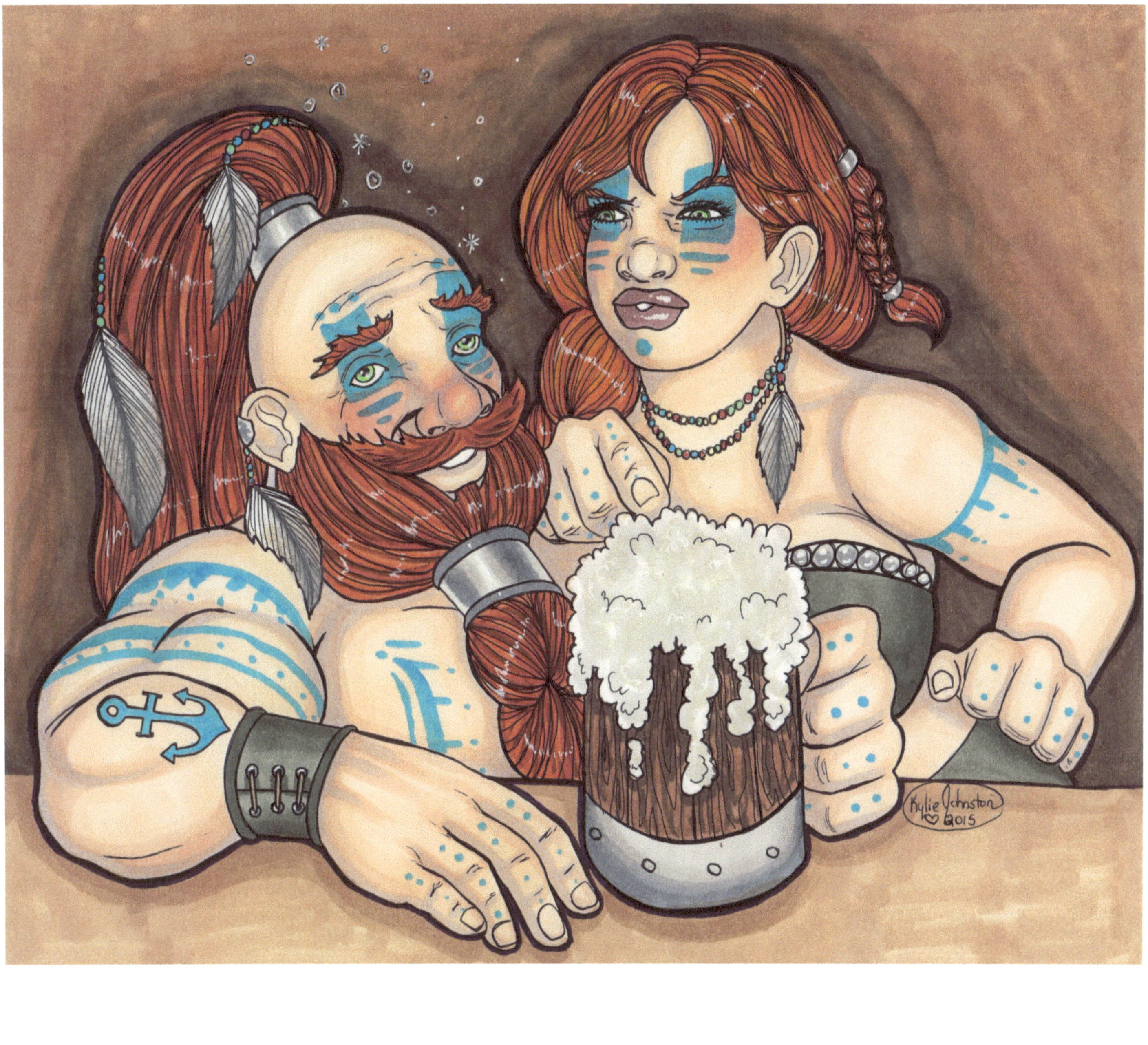

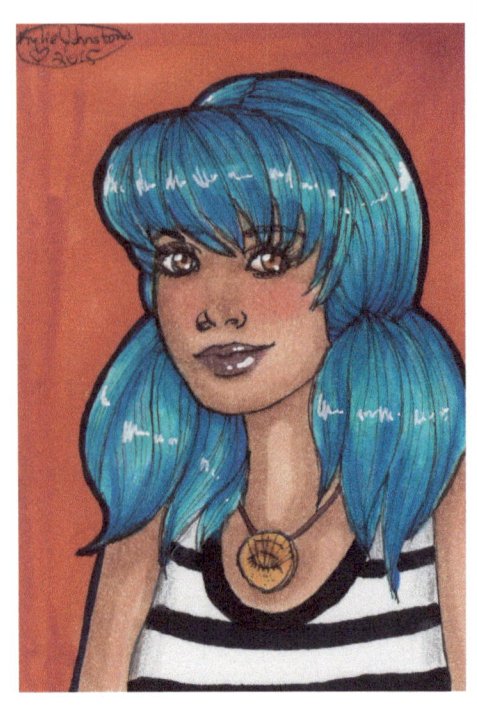
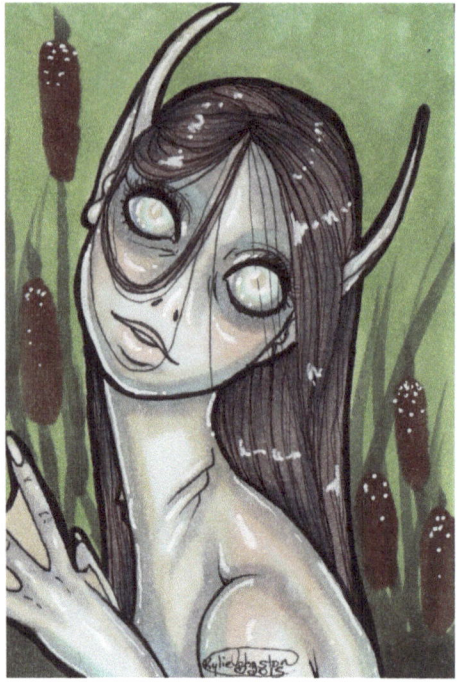
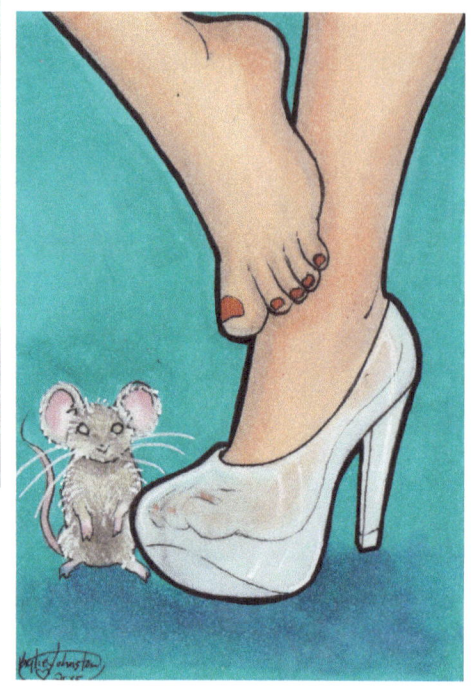
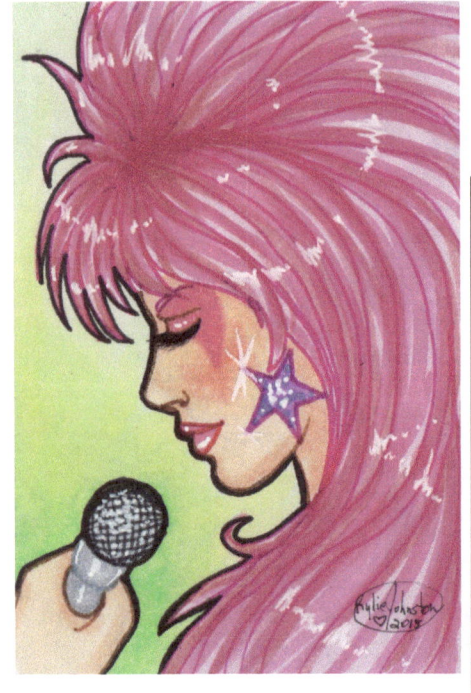
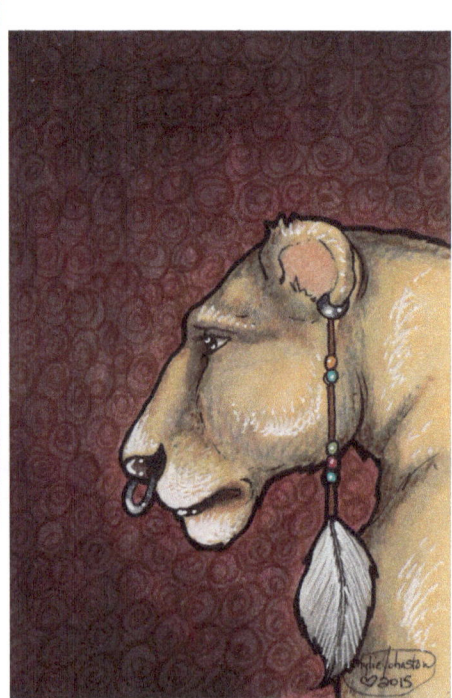
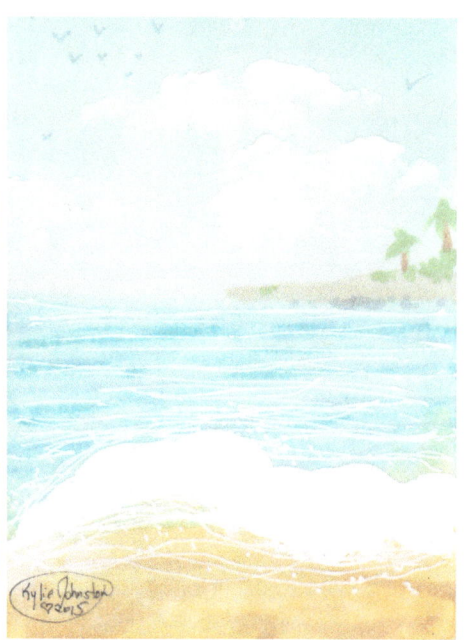

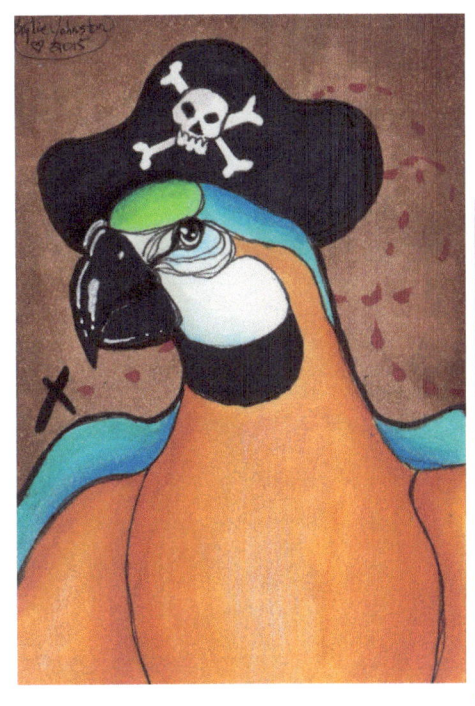
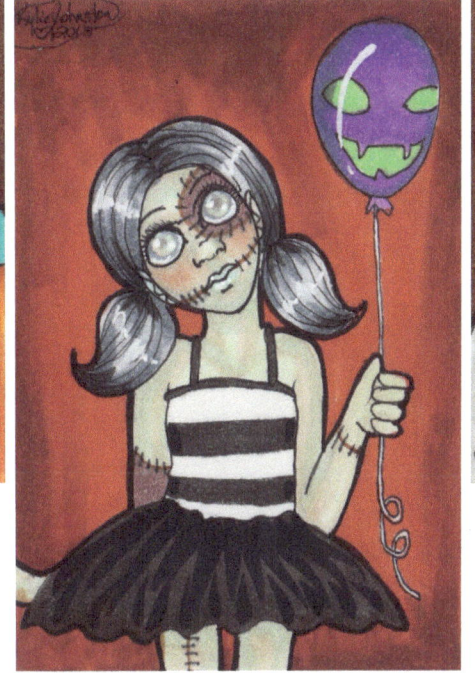
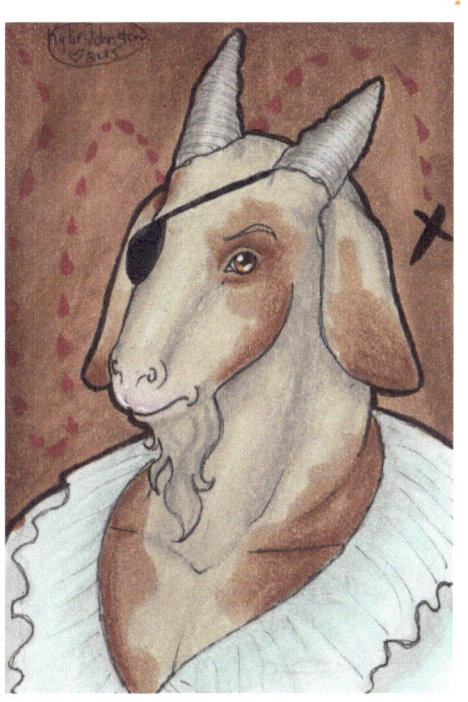
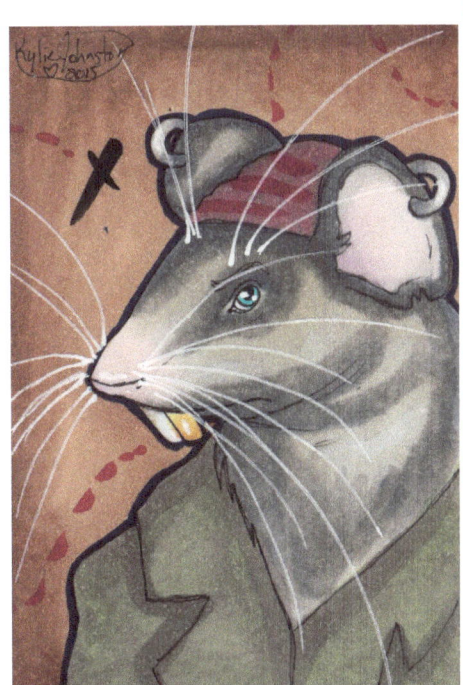
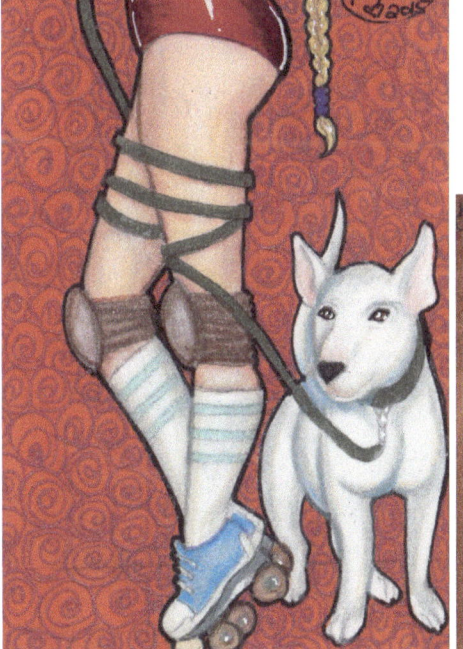
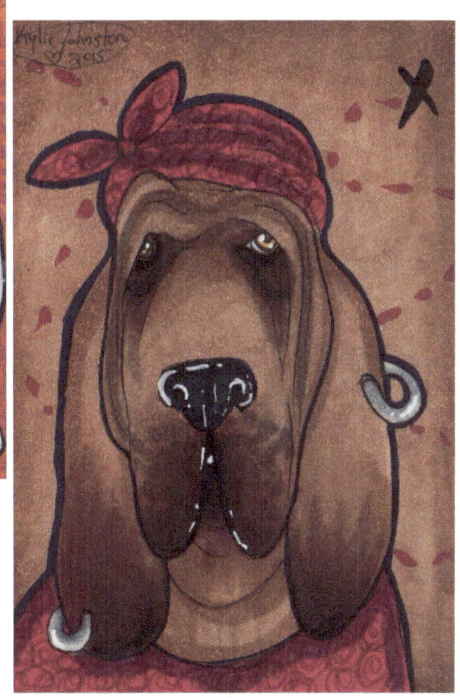

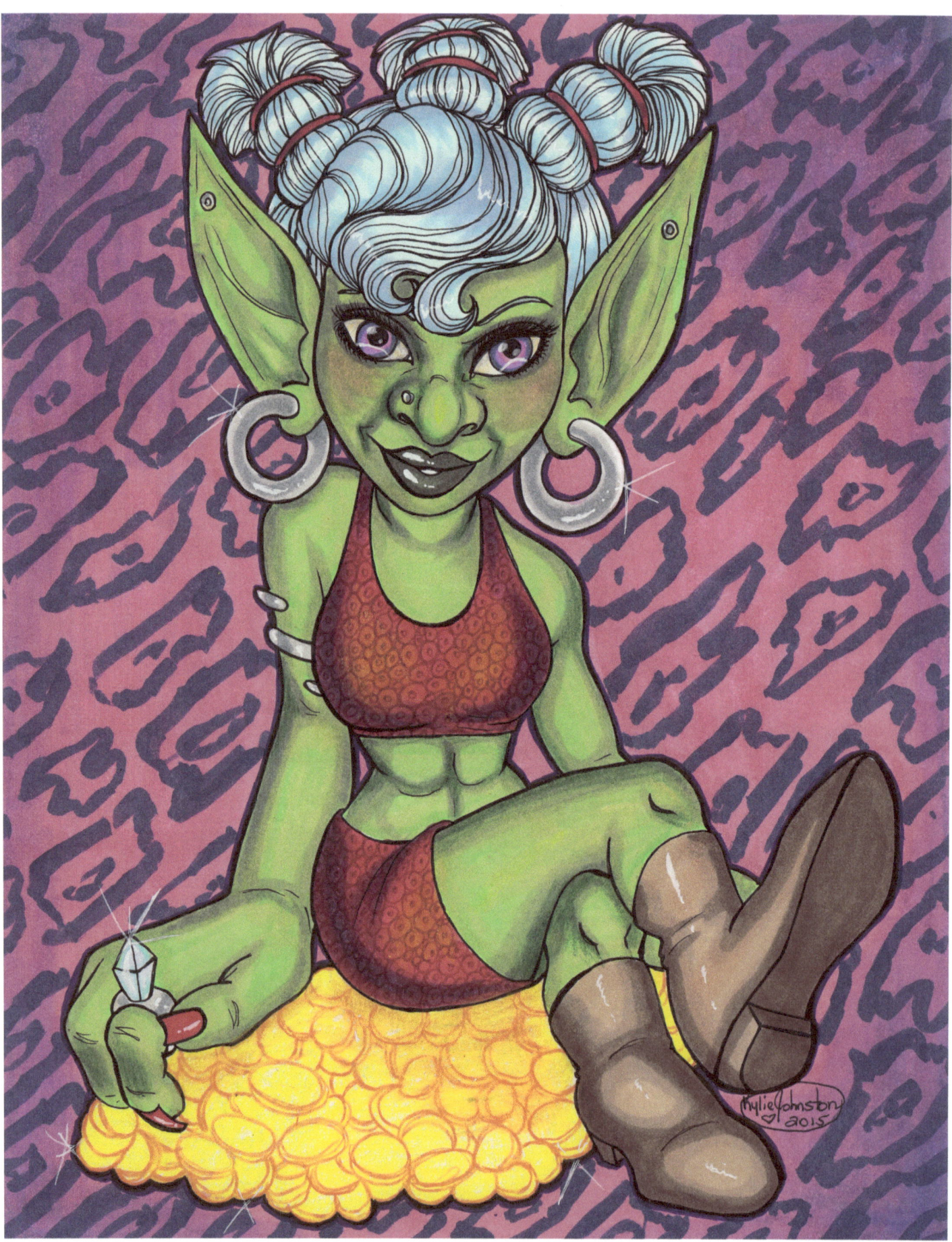

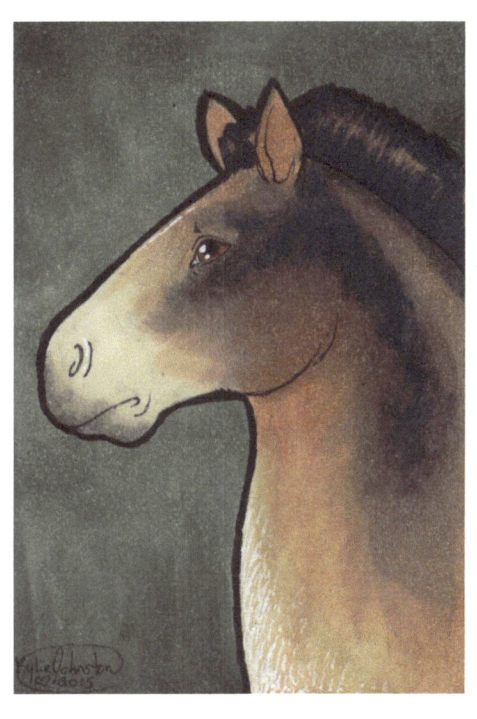
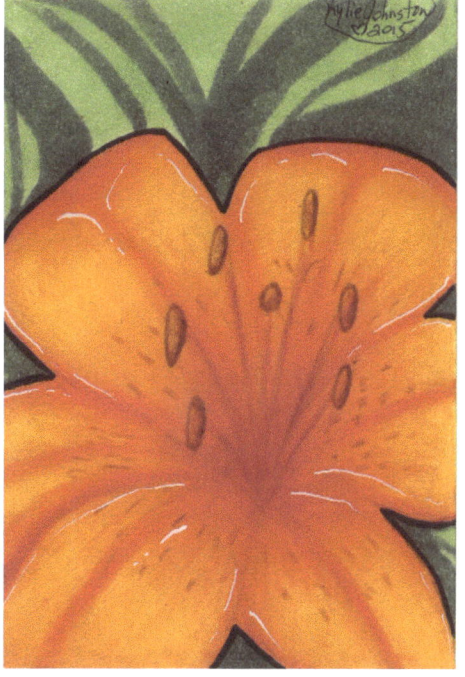
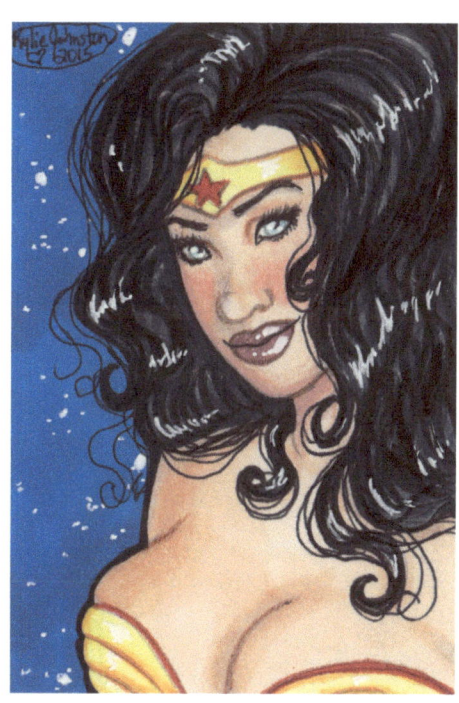
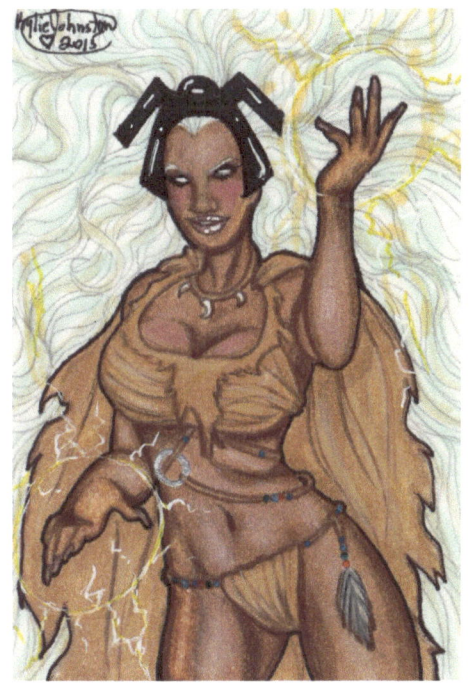
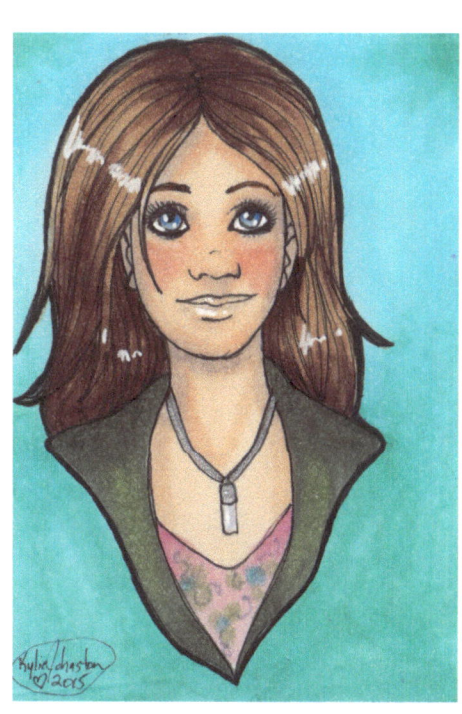
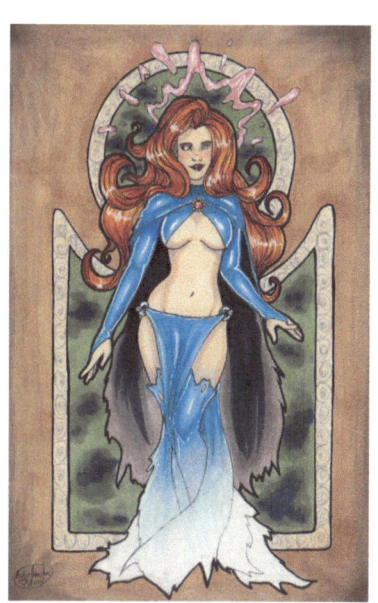

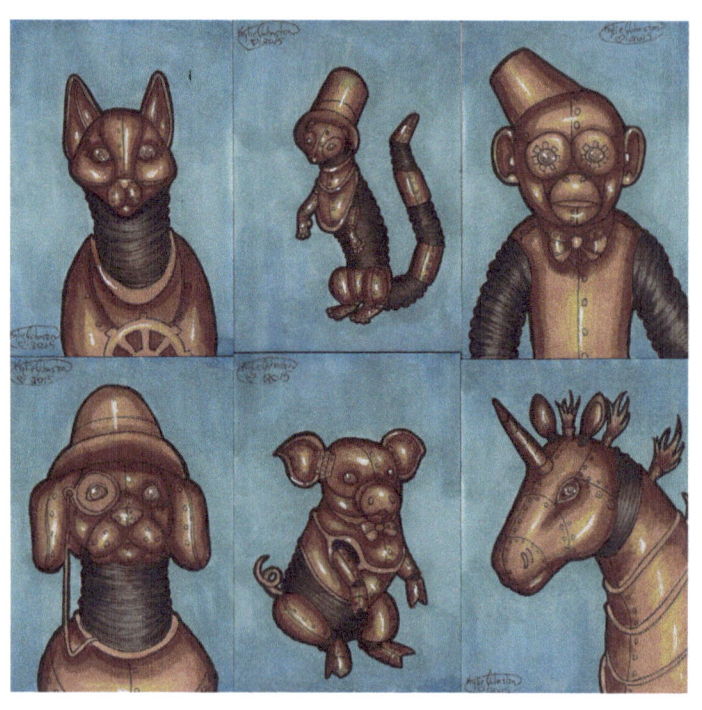

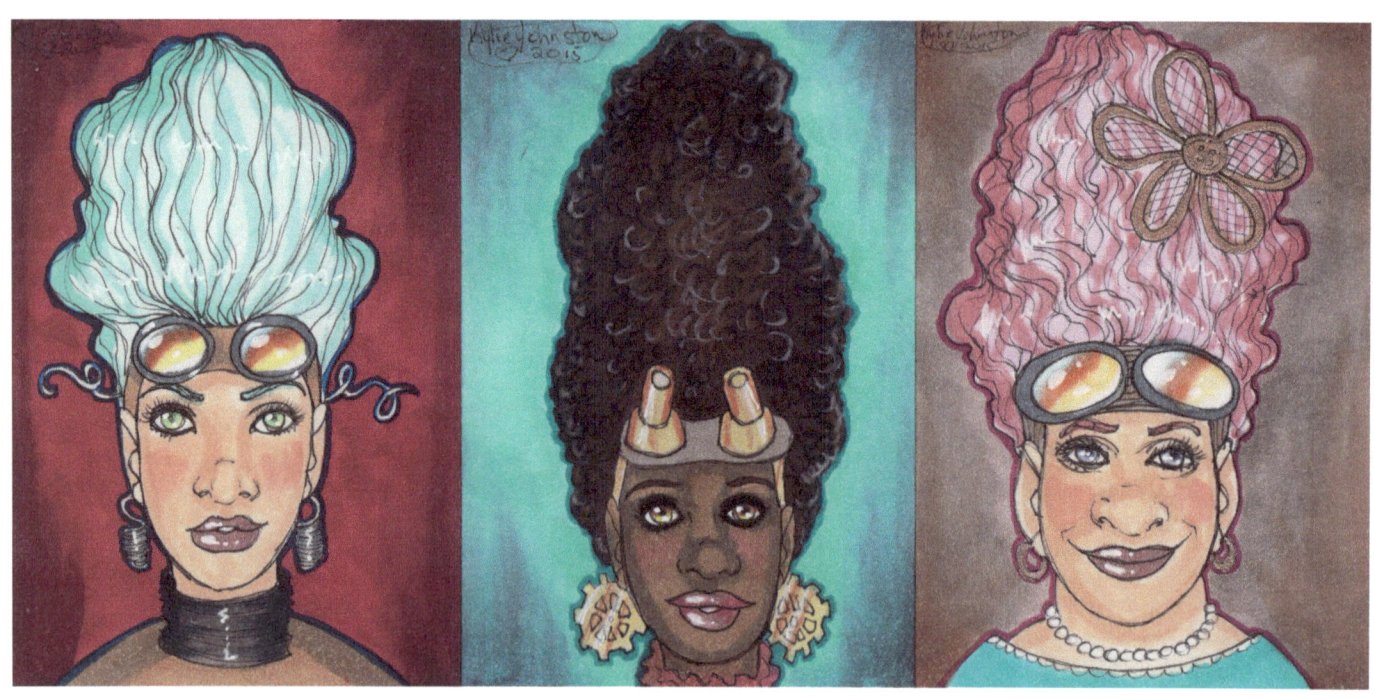

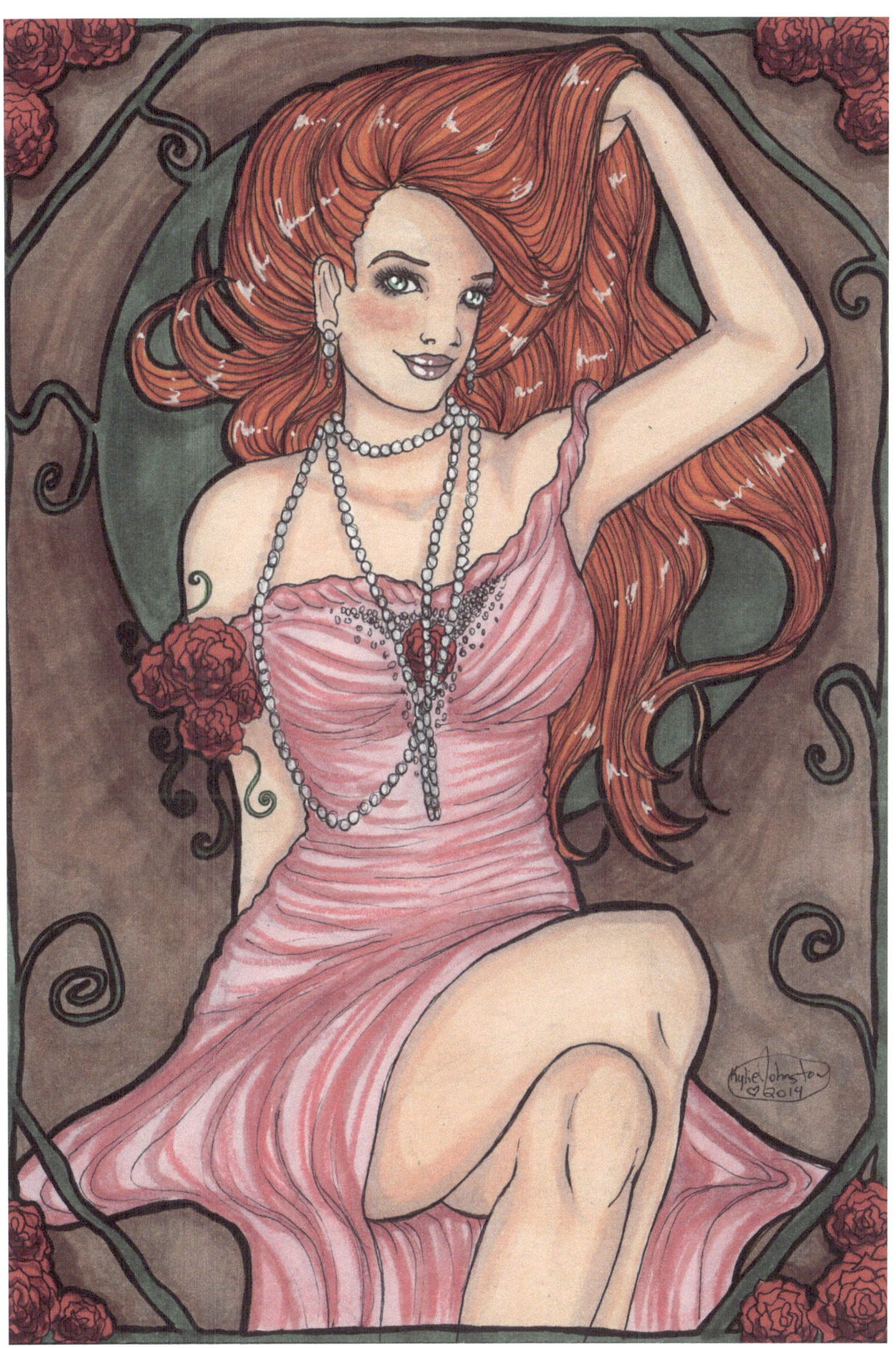

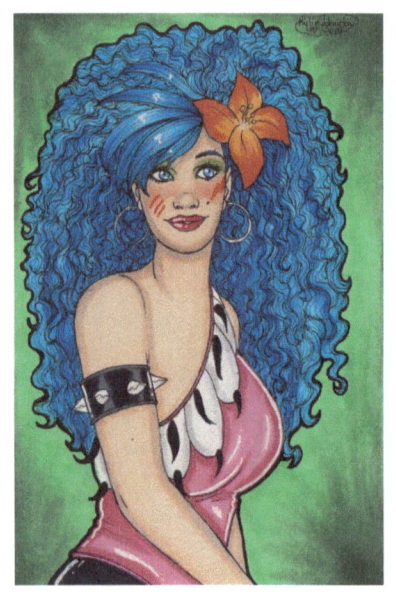
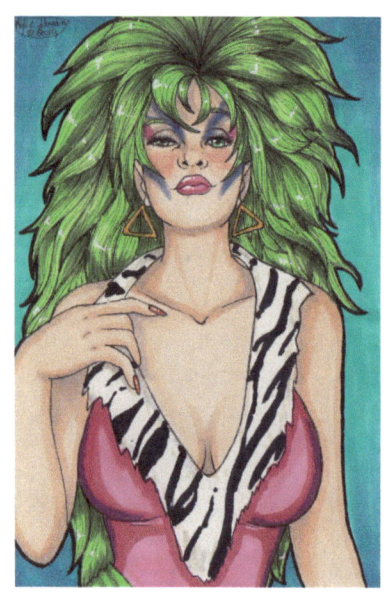
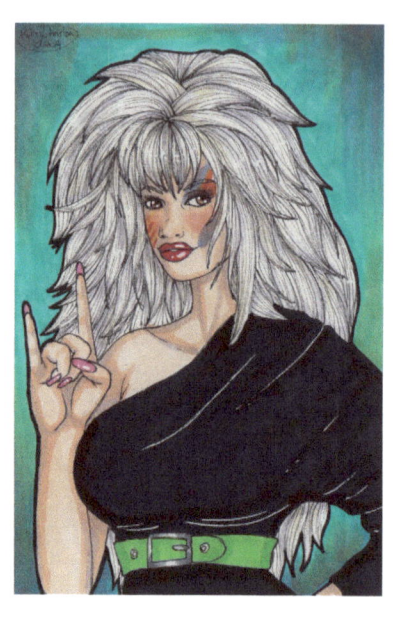
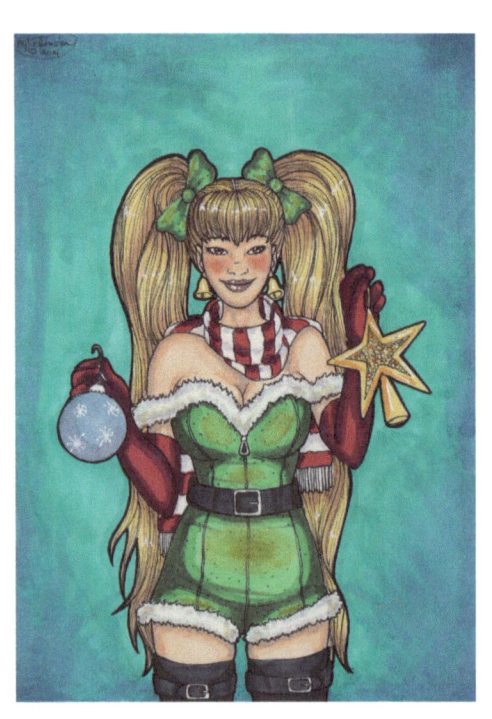
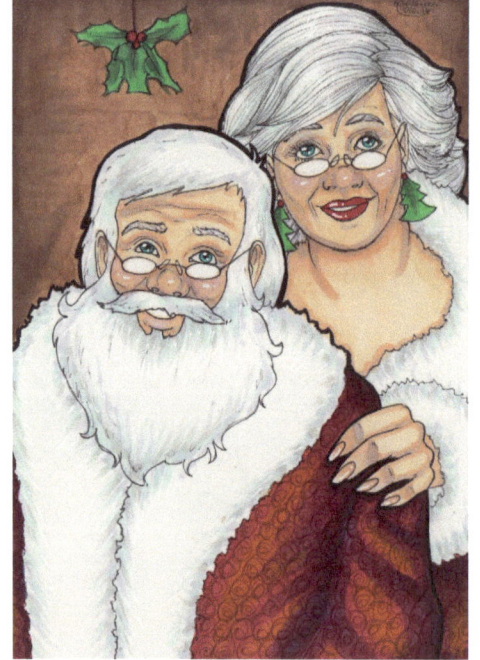
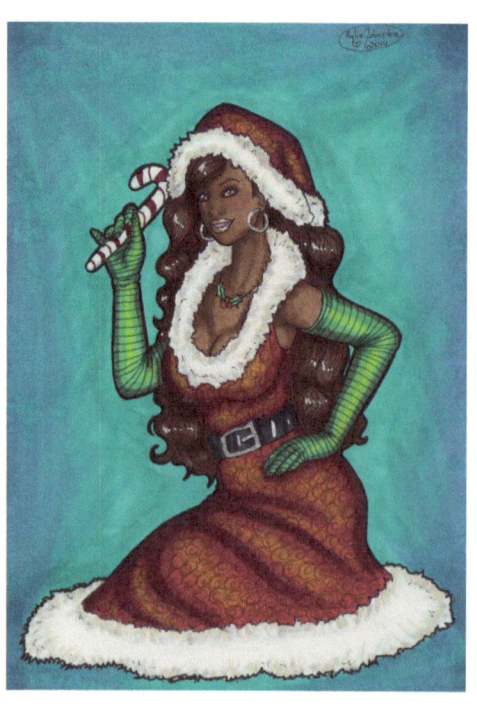

2000–2013

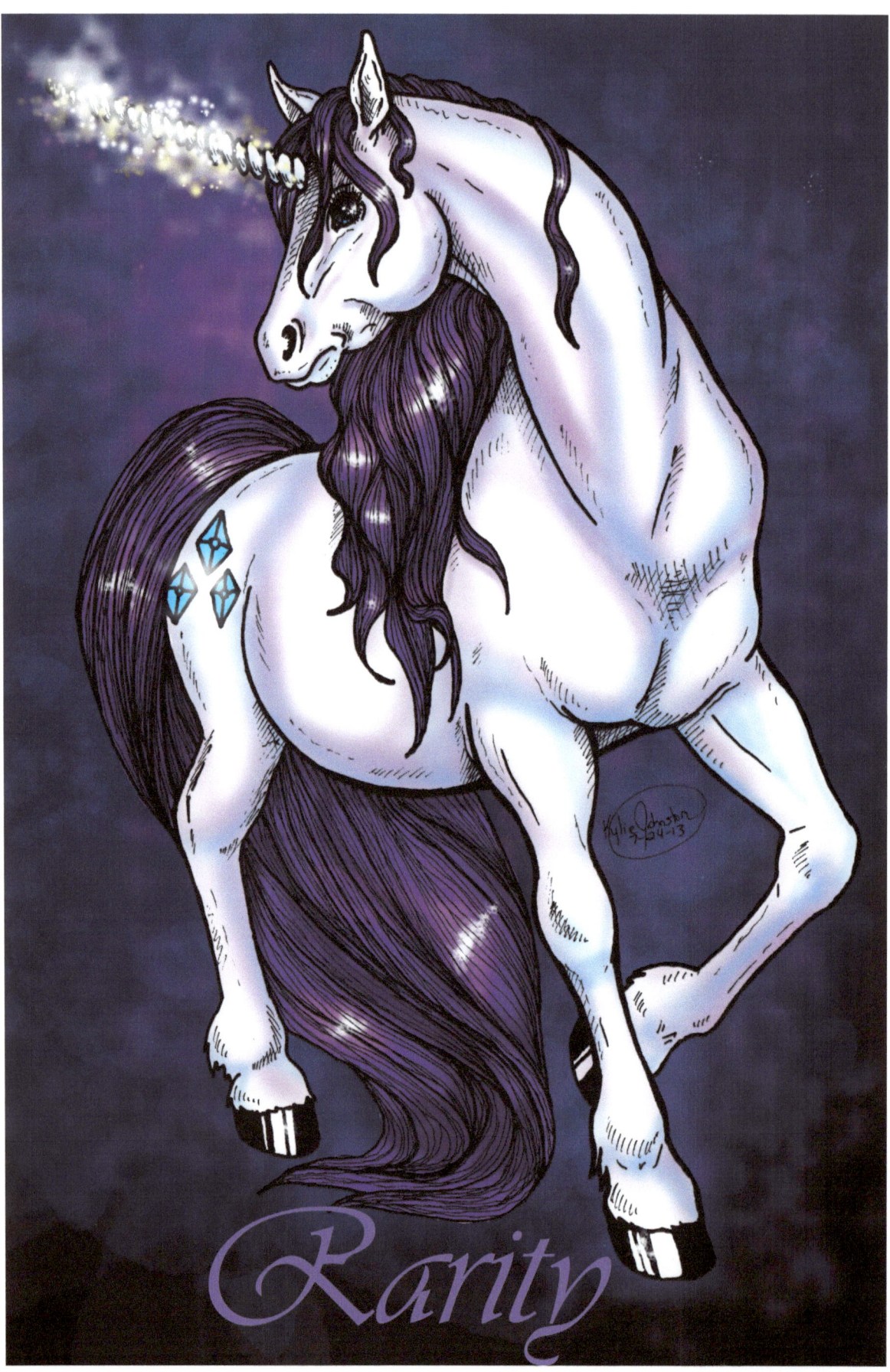

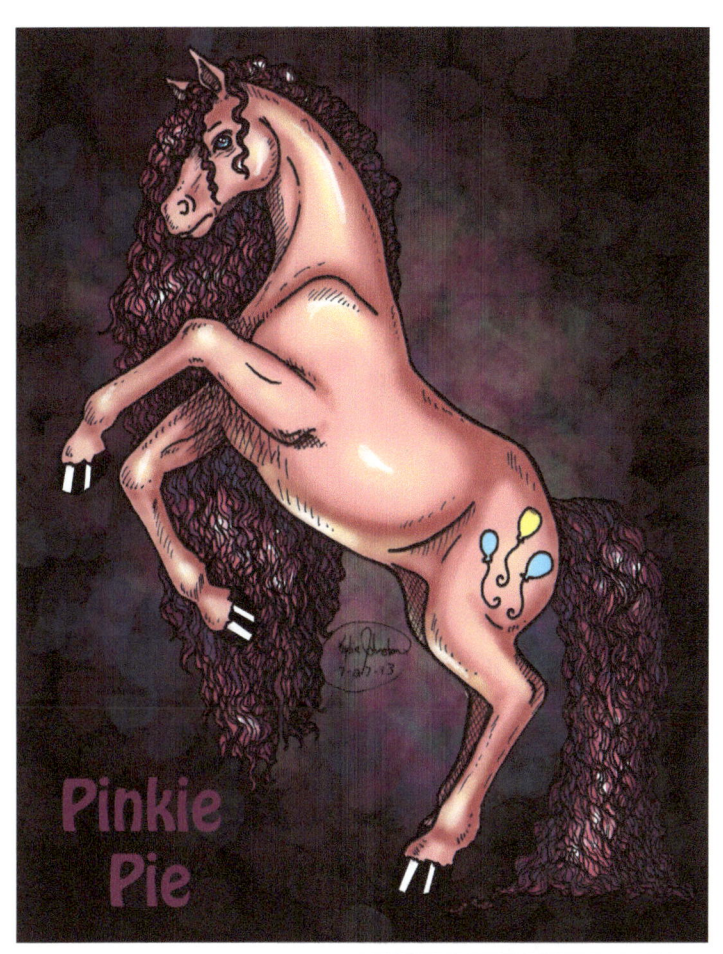

Pinkie
Pie

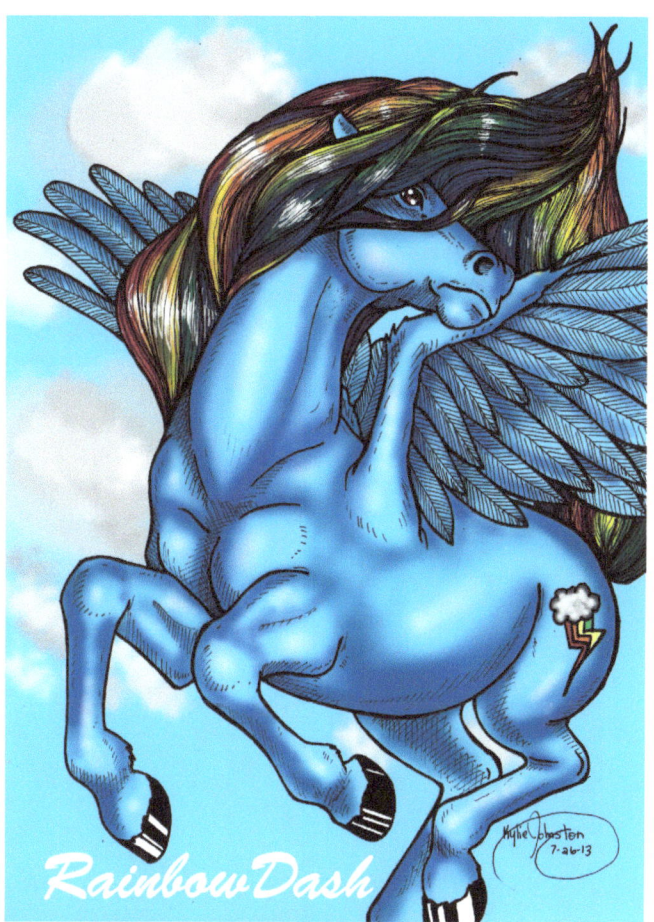

RainbowDash

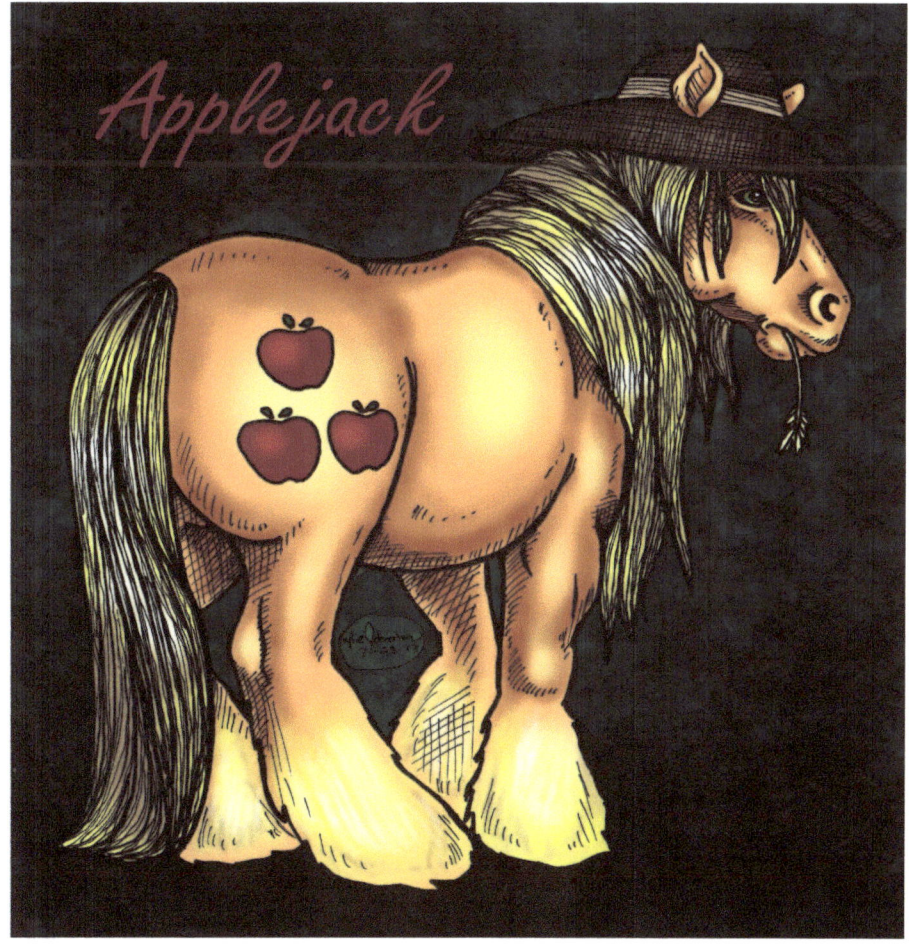

Applejack

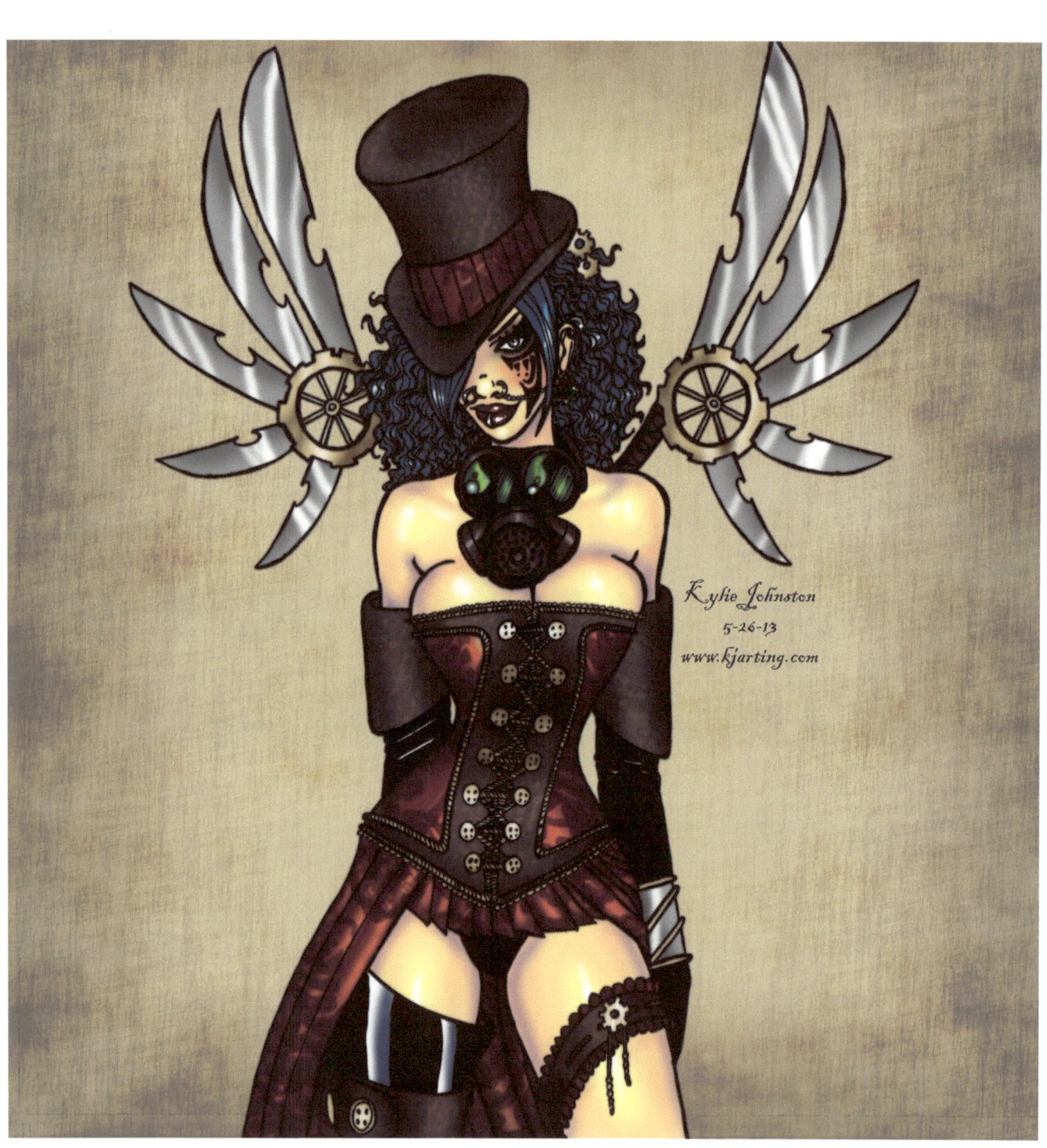

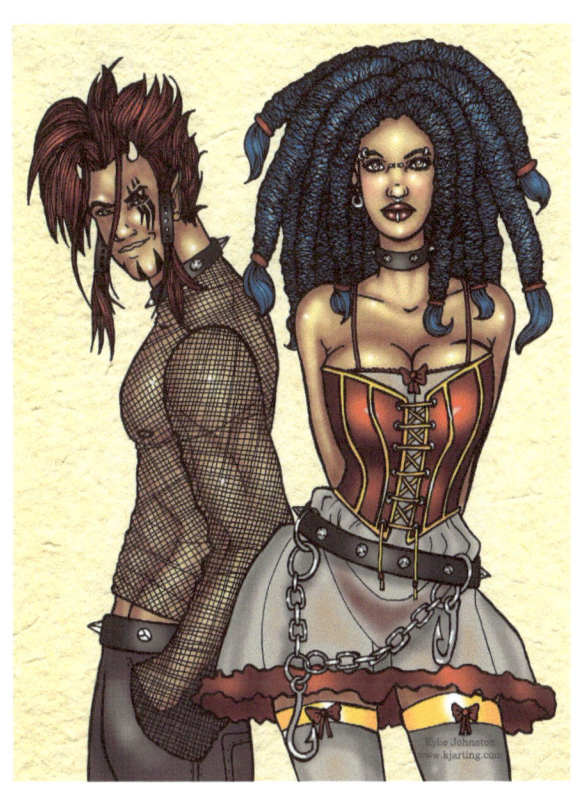

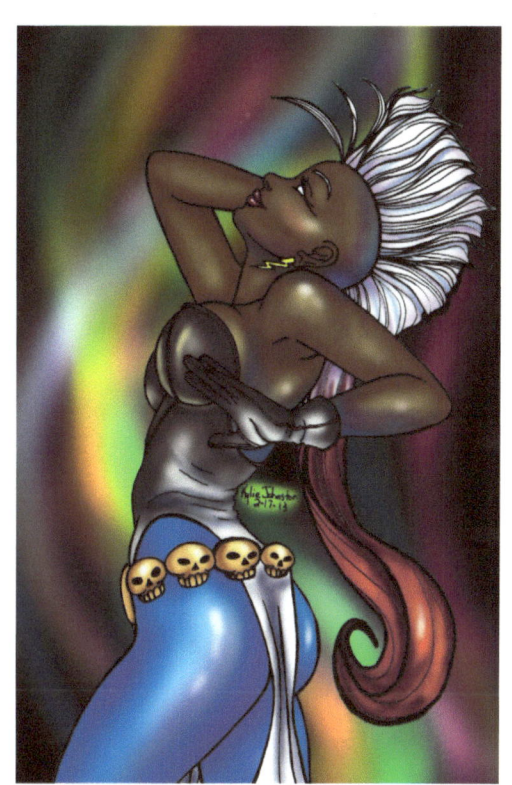

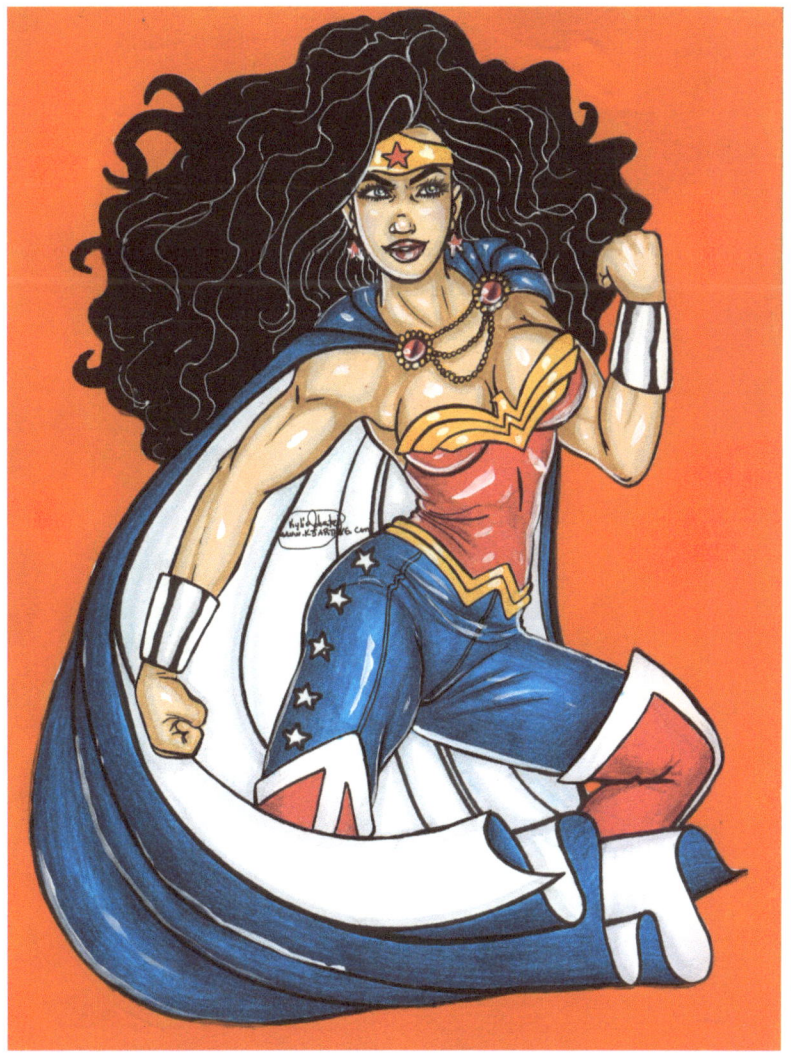

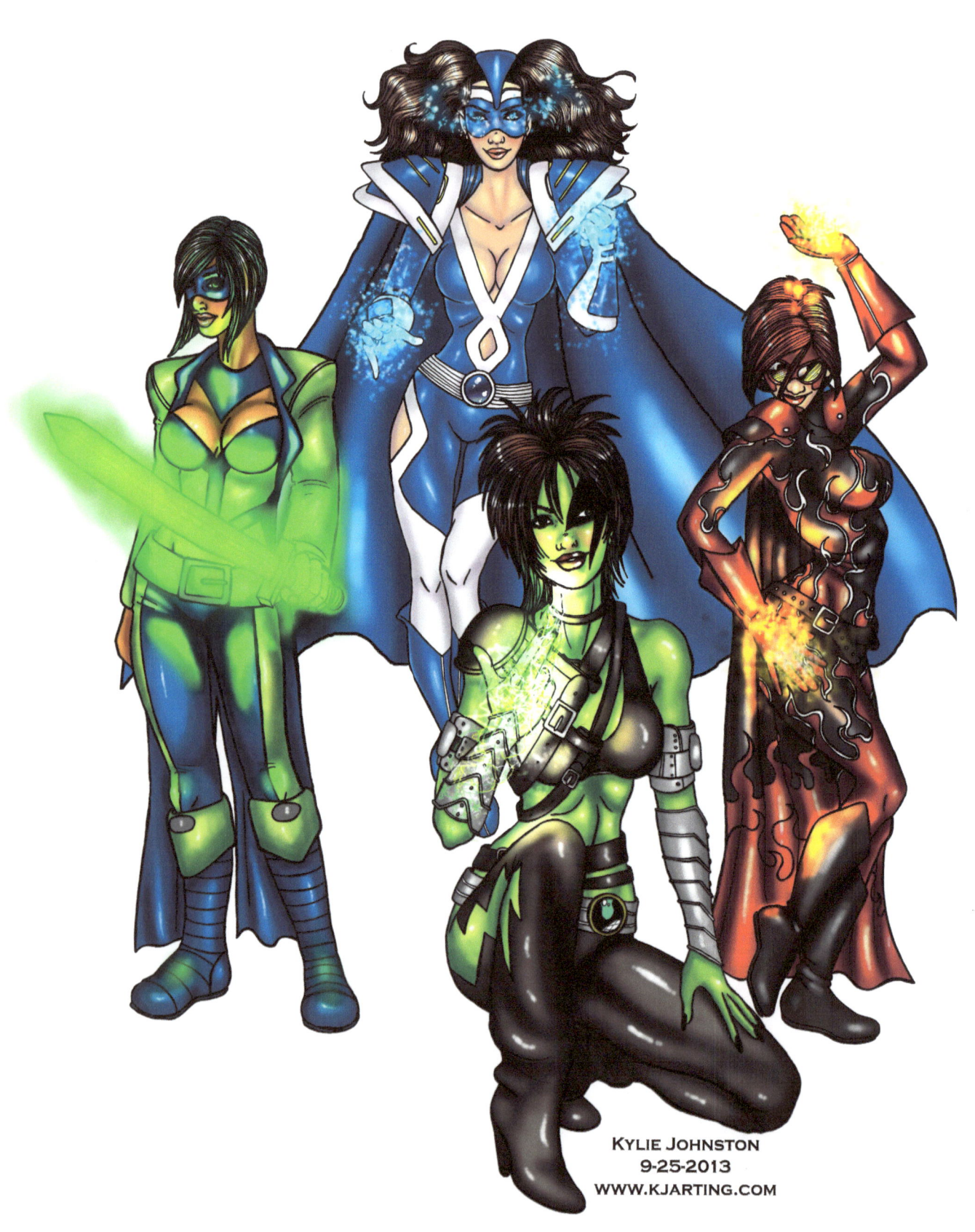

KYLIE JOHNSTON
9-25-2013
WWW.KJARTING.COM

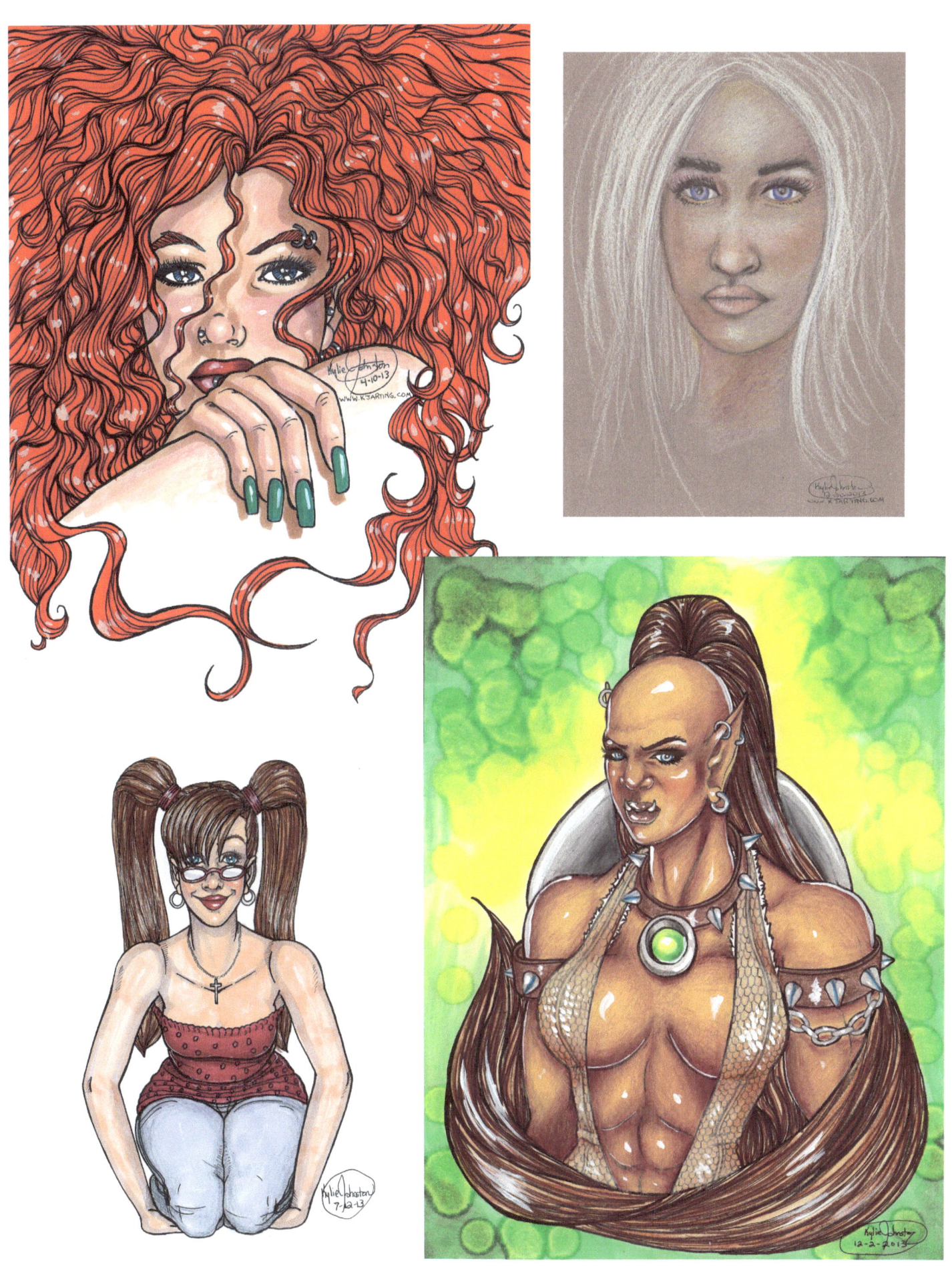

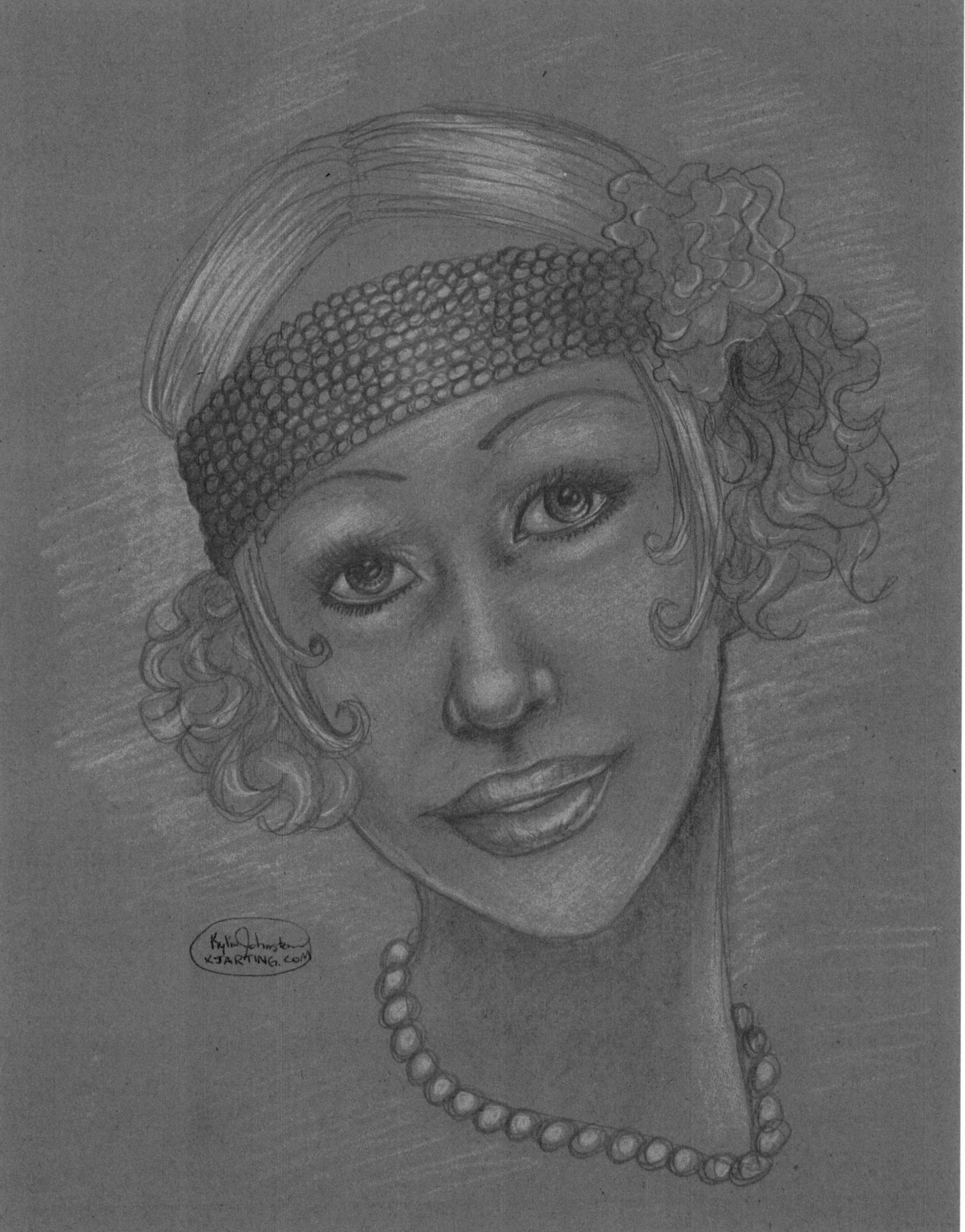

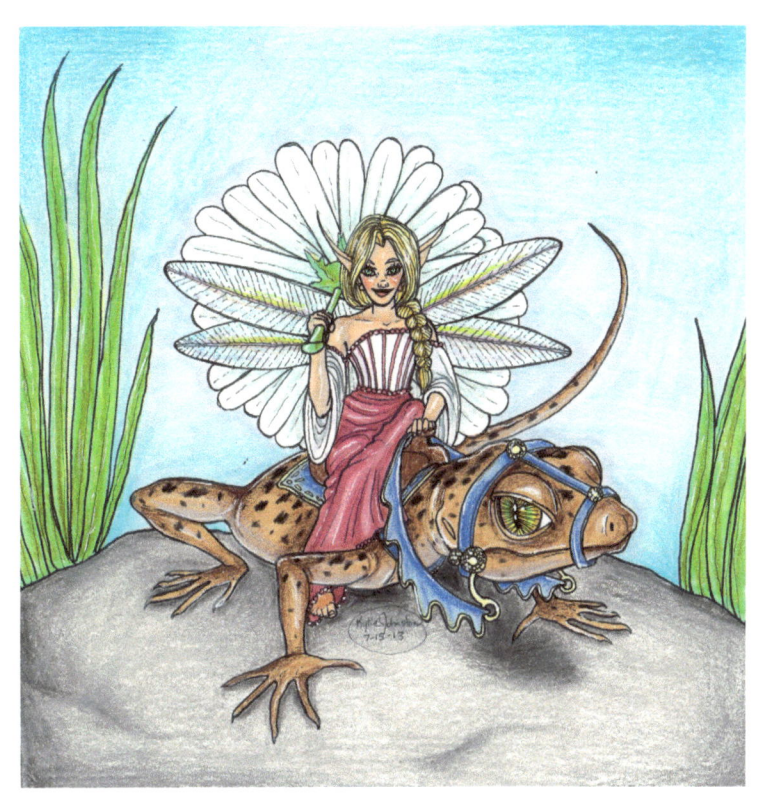

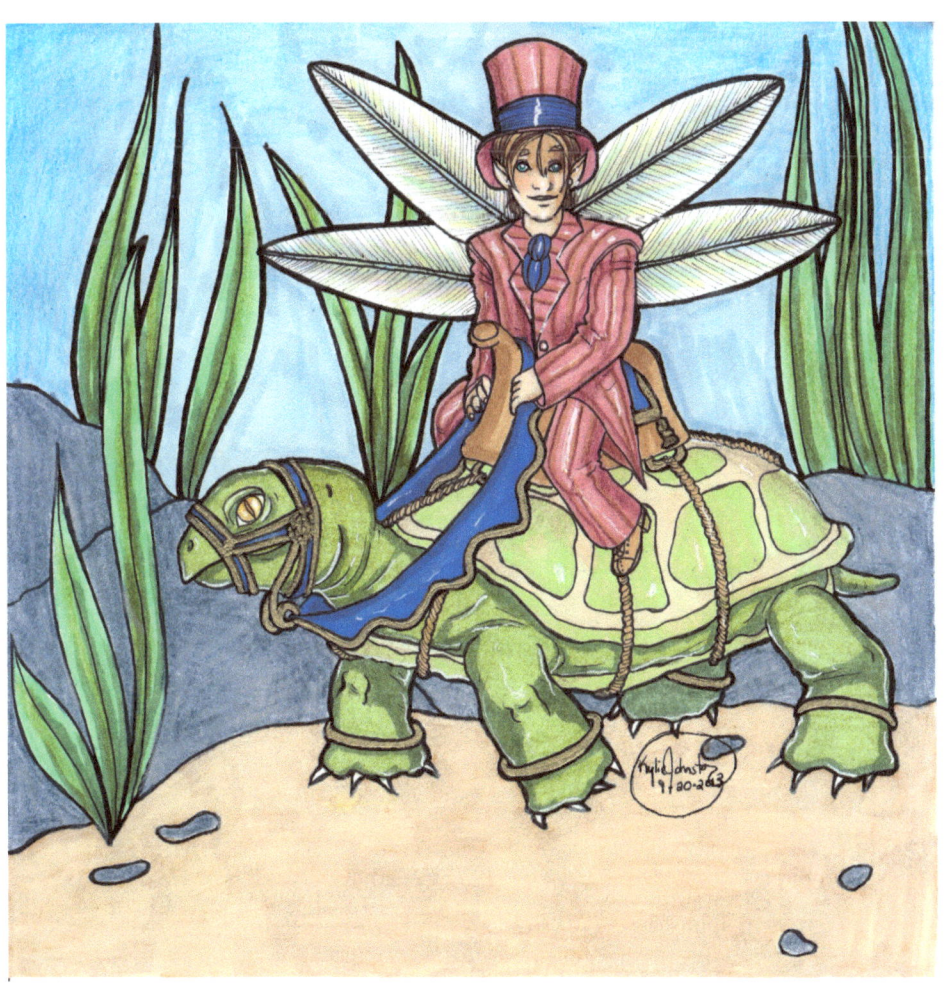

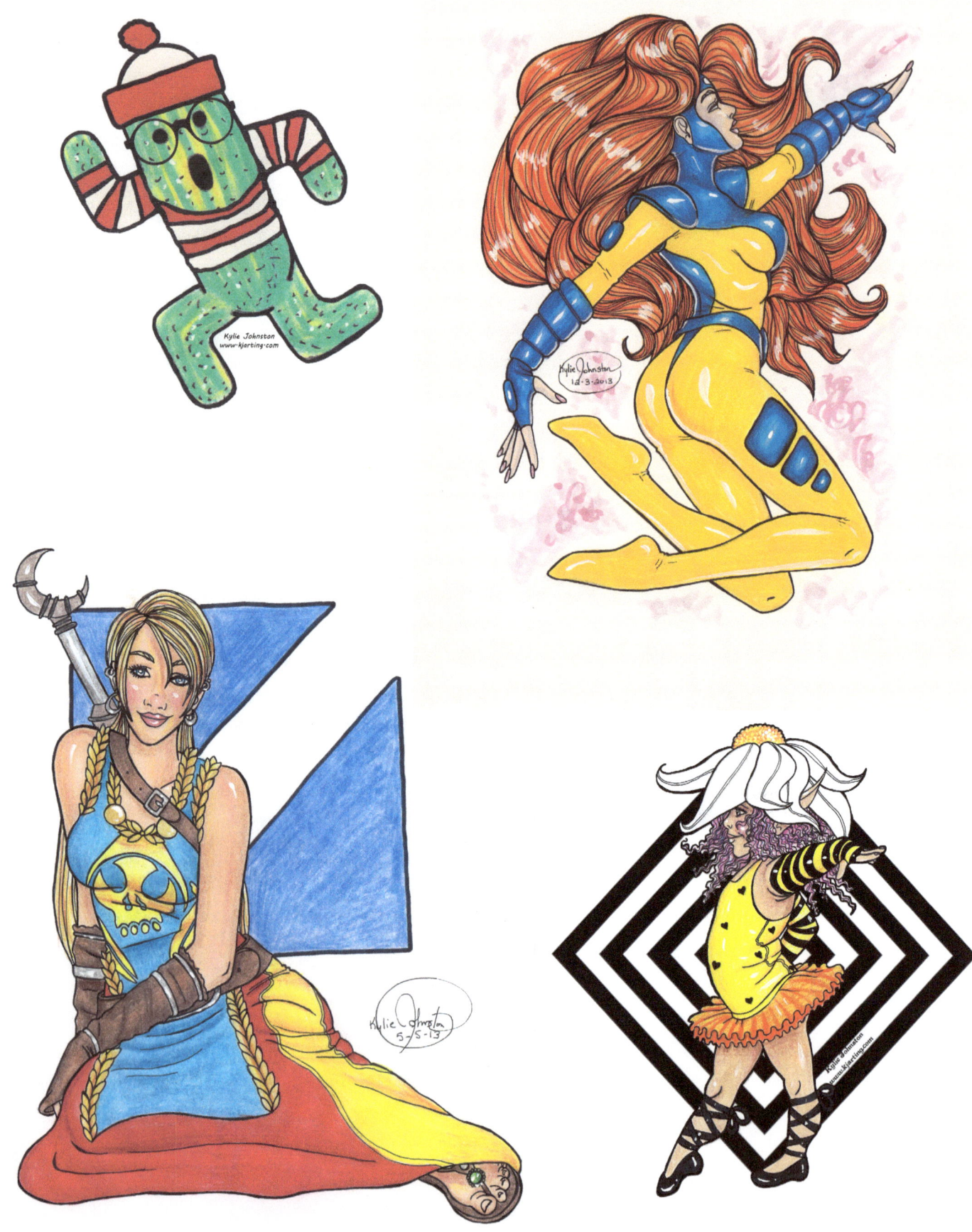

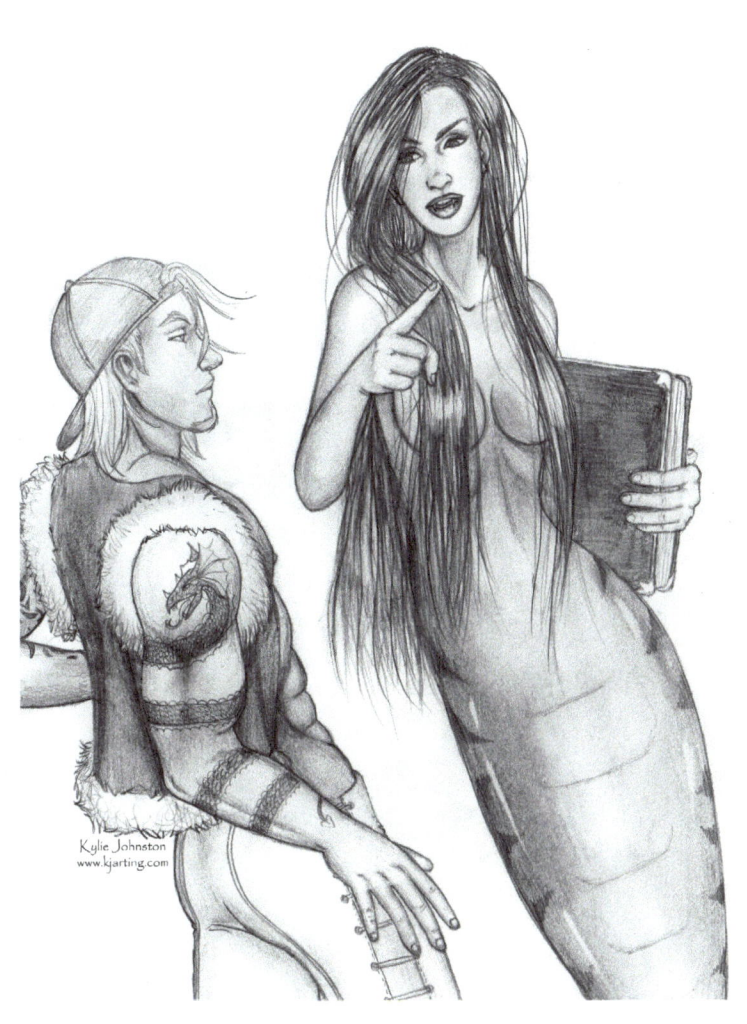

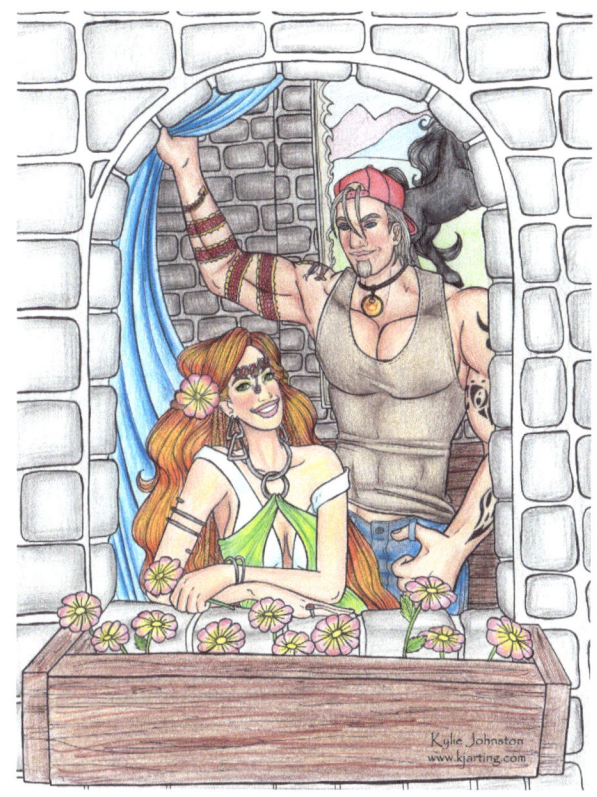

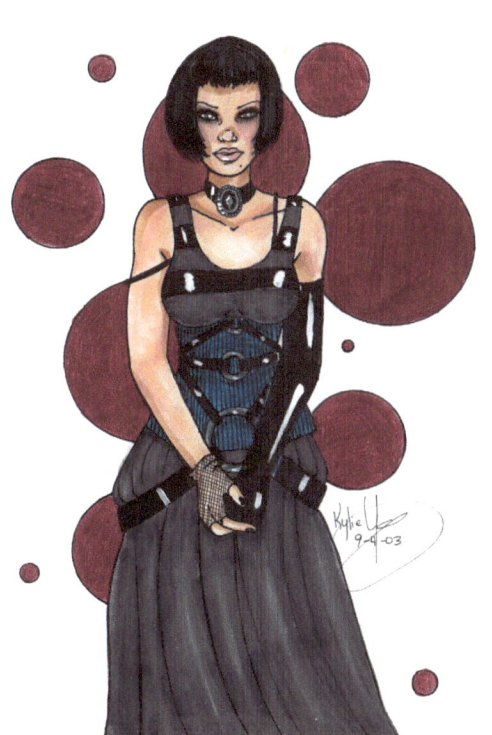

BLITZ OFF!

COME SEE YOUR
FAVORITE
TEAMS!

BESAID
AUROCHS

AL BHED
PSYCHES

GUADO
GLORIES

RONSO
FANGS

AND MORE!

PLAYER OF
THE YEAR
NAIDA!

LUCA
STADIUM

YEVON CUP
TOURNAMENT!

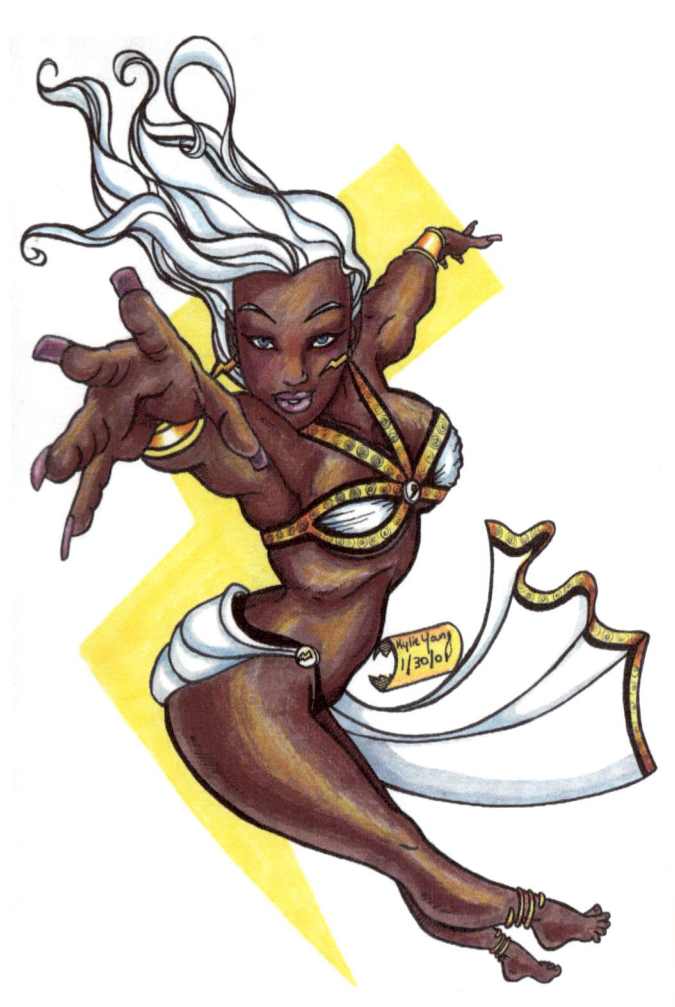
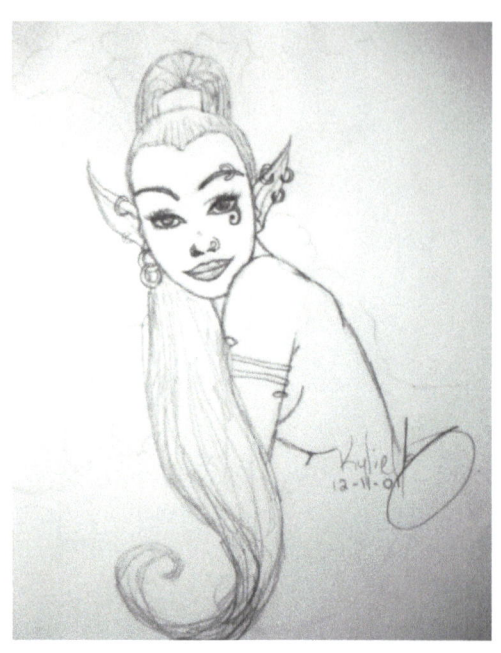
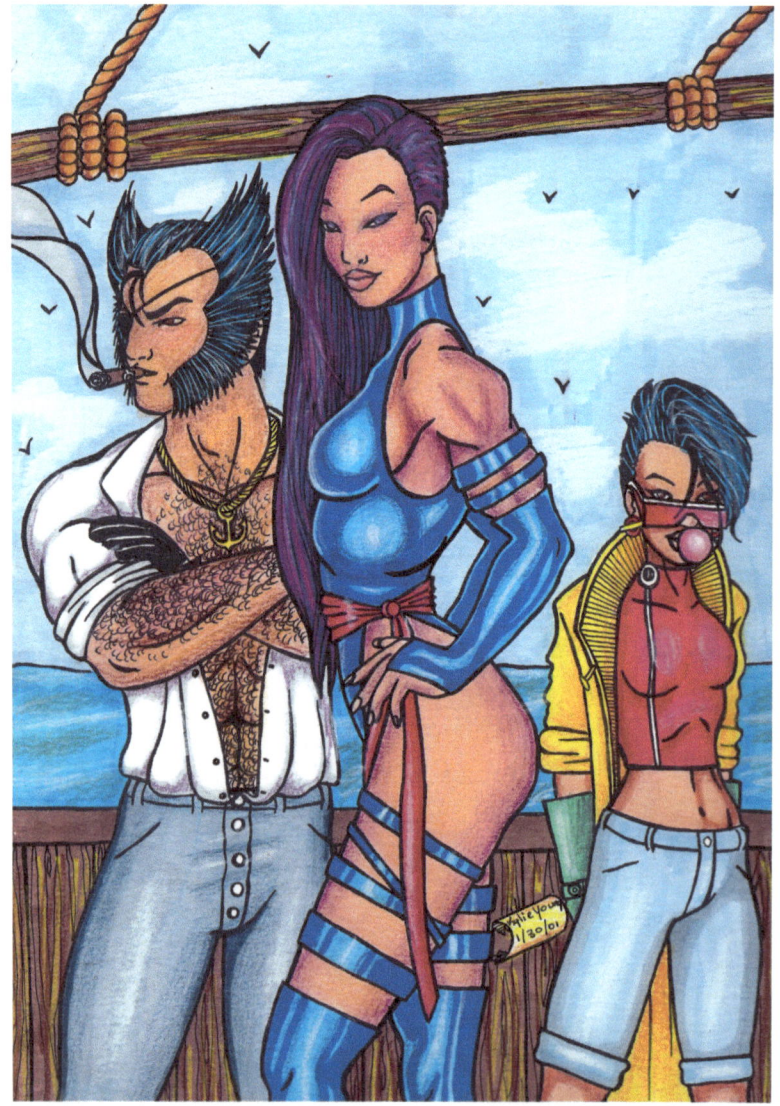